MW01115250

DO YOU KNOW
S CLUB 7-SPEAK?

Instead of Saying:	They Say:
He's very attractive	*He's sooooo Leo*
Go away	*Bore off*
Hey, aren't you listening?	*Earth to*
No way	*No in those heels*
Obviously	*Obv*
In the dog house	*In the hamster cage*

ST. MARTIN'S PAPERBACKS TITLES
BY ANNA LOUISE GOLDEN

'N Sync

Five

Brandy

Backstreet Boys

The Moffatts

*B*Witched*

Jennifer Love Hewitt

Christina Aguilera

Sugar Ray

S club 7

ANNA LOUISE GOLDEN

St. Martin's Paperbacks

S CLUB 7

ISBN: 0-312-97654-2

Printed in the United States of America

St. Martin's Paperbacks edition / September 2000

10 9 8 7 6 5 4 3 2 1

ACKNOWLEDGMENTS

IT'S IMPOSSIBLE for me to even think of a book without thinking of Madeleine Morel, my remarkable agent, and without whom this might never have happened. Not merely this book, but my entire career—I'm in her debt. And Glenda Howard, who got behind this (and many other) ideas, pushing them into reality—you, too, are a marvel.

While a writer always does work alone, there's always a network of people to back her up. In my case Kevin Odell gets the prize this time around, for mailing me stuff from England, and never, ever losing his cred. Also various magazine editors who are always understanding when I'm in the midst of a book. But none of this would have worked without the love and support of L&G. Sometimes I feel like there's an angel on my shoulder and buttercups around my feet. Thanks to everyone.

The following all proved very helpful in the writing of this book: *S Club 7 in Miami: The Official Scrapbook*, by Jeremy Mark (Harper Entertainment, 1999); *Top of the Pops*, December 1999; *Top of the Pops*, October 1999; "Daydream Relievers," by Victoria Neal, *Entrepreneur*, November 1999; *Smash Hits*, December 1, 1999; *On Top of the World*, supplement to *Top of the Pops*; "We're Puttin' on the Brits," *Teen Beat*, February 2000.

INTRODUCTION

BY NOW, you know there's no party quite like an S Club party. And you also know you're all invited. It's a British thing, loose and free, and a lot of fun. Four girls, three guys, a lot of music, singing, dancing, jokes, and a time to remember. It's not just a party for a Saturday night, it's a party for your whole life.

But then again, fun is in the blood for Jon, Jo, Rachel, Hannah, Bradley, Tina, and Paul. Whether at home in England, when they first got together, in Italy, where they initially rehearsed, in Miami—where they made their show, of course—or in Los Angels, where they've been filming another show, it's all been about having loads of fun while they worked.

And work is something they've done almost without a break since they first got together. In Miami, for example, it was every single day for more than two months as they filmed the first season of *S Club 7 in Miami*, which has been such a hit on the Fox Family Channel. How big a hit? Well, when the channel showed a marathon, and gave a toll-free number for people to call in for a free S Club 7 record, they received a totally incredible seven *million* requests.

It's remarkable, really, that seven people can get along so well together when they see each other every day (just think of what happens in *The Real World* for comparison), but right from the start everyone in S Club 7 has hit it off as if they'd always been friends. Even when they're all completely stressed (and you try working every day and not getting stressed), there haven't been arguments or tantrums. No one has pulled star trips. They're like the Musketeers—all for one and one for all.

It would be enough if they'd just starred in a show that many compared, for its humor and music, to *The Monkees* back in the sixties. But S Club 7 are also a major recording act. In England they've enjoyed three hit singles (their third, "You're My Number One/Two In A Million," was number two at the start of the new millennium), as well as an album that's just shot out of the stores, and a home video that's been amazingly popular since its release. And you just know America's going to go exactly the same way.

They've introduced a lot of British slang terms to a generation of Americans—who in the United States knew what "parp" was before S Club came along? (It means rubbish, garbage, just in case you weren't already familiar.) But that's one of the beauties of the show. It doesn't try to make any of them into people they're not; they're simply being themselves on camera, talking and sounding just the way they would at home.

It's pop music, but everyone knows there's nothing wrong with good pop music. It can make you feel like you're on top of the world. A good song can bring back some of the best moments of your life. And that's what S Club 7 do.

It's no secret that the band was put together. Unlike a lot of groups, they didn't link up on their own, then appear out of nowhere. It was Simon Fuller and his company, 19 Management, that had the idea for the band and arranged all the auditions. He had plenty of experience in the field, having previously managed one of the world's biggest bands, the Spice Girls, not to mention the careers of a number of other people in the entertainment and sports field (Steve McManaman, who plays soccer for Liverpool, the team Mel C. vocally supports, is one of his clients). But having hit once doesn't automatically mean you'll hit again. Even selecting seven candidates who seem perfect is no guarantee of a chemistry between the people. He was lucky, because all seven have got along so well. And, by the very nature of the business, a couple of them did already know each other— Hannah and Paul were mates, having worked together at the National Youth Music Theatre.

It helps that they all had plenty of experience, that they were professionals in their fields. Jo had been a singer, a country singer in fact, while others had acted. Jon Lee had been in *EastEnders*, one of the top British soap operas (ironically enough, he's a major fan of *EastEnders*' biggest soap rival, *Coronation Street*, and made his parents tape every episode for him while he was away filming in Miami). The only one who really didn't have much professional experience was Rachel, who'd been working in public relations.

But whatever they'd done, it couldn't have prepared them for all the intensity of being a part of S Club 7. No sooner were they all selected than they were off to Italy, of all places, to start rehearsing (nice work if you can get it, right?). For two weeks they worked day and night with arrangers and choreographers, going over songs and dances again and again. In part they'd been chosen because they could be quick studies, and because they showed real acting ability. Finding seven people who could sing, dance, *and* act wasn't easy, but this lot had it all going on.

Once they were back home, there were a few shows to let people see them, and so they could get out on stage together and experience working as a band. Once all that had been worked out, it was into the recording studio to make an album. Only Jo had recorded her own song before (she'd actually had a hit single in Germany). The pressure was intense, because as soon as their studio time was up, they were jetting off to Florida to start work on the series—no rest for the wicked!

A lot of people would have cracked under that kind of workload, but Paul, Rachel, Hannah, Bradley, Jon, Tina, and Jo were all hungry and resilient. Give them a day to acclimate themselves to the sun and sand (another tough job!), and they were good to go.

There were thirteen episodes to be filmed. And they had to be done in a little over two months, which meant far more than one episode a week. And *that* was real work. Days in television tend to run long anyway, usually at least twelve hours, but these were going past that. Every single day. Well, okay, there was the occasional (very occasional) bit of time off for good behavior, when the gang would head to the trendy South Beach area of Miami to shop and go clubbing. But those times were rare.

Although the title was *S Club 7 in Miami*, most of the time they really weren't in Miami at all, but Lauderdale by the Sea, much smaller and easier for filming. However, the Florida Paradise Hotel of the series was their real home while they were filming (art getting mixed up with life). Its real name, though, isn't Florida Paradise, but Villas by the Sea, and residents were there while all the filming was going on—in fact, several of them had walk-on parts!

It was all-comedy, all-singing, all-dancing. And that meant all the songs had to be shot several times, from different angles. When you consider that over the course of the series there were fifteen songs, that's even more work.

And just in case you think the show was all the guys and girls just talking, it was written by people who'd previously worked on shows like *Friends, Fresh Prince of Bel Air*, as well as the British sitcom *Red Dwarf* (a favorite on PBS) and *Spiceworld: The Movie*. In other words, the writers had some pretty major credits, but it was due to the ability of the Club and the others that it felt so natural.

But Jon, Bradley, Jo, Tina, Rachel, Paul, and Hannah weren't the only singing stars on the set. Jill Ward, the actress Jon got to know in one episode and who befriended the band, was played by Cathy Dennis, who had a huge voice and who had enjoyed international hits. No end of talent on the show.

For most of the Club, Florida was their first experience of America, and they loved it. But it wouldn't be their last by any means. Even when the filming was done, they'd be back. And they'd end up returning even sooner than they imagined, to the other warm American paradise—Los Angeles. They were to film a special for British television called *Back to the Fifties*, and since the fifties had been all about America and rock 'n' roll (Britain in the fifties had been a very gray place), what better than to film it in America, to go to the source?

Add to that some concerts, including an appearance at Party In The Park, the Prince's Trust charity benefit in London's Hyde Park, singing to 100,000 people, and you've got a very busy year indeed. Not too surprisingly, that particular performance was probably the most nerve-wracking they'd ever experienced—and certainly the biggest crowd they'd ever had.

And finally *S Club 7 in Miami* hit television around the world in the fall of 1999. In Britain the band was already known, thanks to the hits it had enjoyed. Elsewhere, though, they were an unknown quantity—but not for long. The show (which had undergone a number of working titles, including *7 in Miami* and *7 Up*) was an immediate smash around the globe, even if the media in general chose to ignore it.

Without a great deal of publicity, it managed to attract viewers. In America, it had a great slot on the Fox Family Channel, and quickly found an audience, who spread the word to their friends. When a marathon of episodes was shown on November 27, 1999, just after Thanksgiving, Interscope, the band's U.S. record label, gave people the chance to call in and receive a free single. The company expected somewhere in the region of twenty thousand calls. Instead they received seven million, enough to make their entire phone system crash. That was an un-precedented response, and made it clear that a lot more people were not only watching but also in love with S Club 7, more than anyone had ever imagined.

What most people hadn't realized, however, was that the Club already had a single out in America. "Bring It All Back," their English debut, which had gone all the way to the top of the charts there, was their first Amer-ican release. The response Interscope got from its TV offer made them decide to bring forward the release date of the S Club 7 album in the U.S. to early 2000. And why not? There were plenty of fans out there. Once they knew a record was available with all the songs from the series, they'd be on it.

Meanwhile, the whole gang was remaining very busy. They'd spent part of the fall filming yet another special, a seasonal that aired in England a couple of weeks before Christmas (look for it Christmas 2000 in the States), and saw the double-sided "You're My Number One/Two In A Million" go all the way to number two in the charts. And then there was all the promotional work around the globe that was lined up.

"We went to San Francisco to do promotion but didn't get to see much of it," said Rachel, "although what we did see was beautiful. We're off to Australia and New Zealand, then New York at some point—we're definitely going to have to schedule in some shopping there!"

Well, that's Rachel—of course she wants to shop! But all of them do, to pick up on the designer labels they can't get so easily at home. But there'll be plenty of chances, given that there's going to be another S Club series, which might well be set somewhere in America again. It will begin airing in the fall, by which time they'll undoubtedly already be superstars all over the globe, repeating the success they've enjoyed in Britain. If the phone calls Interscope has received are anything to judge by, then in a few months they'll be huge in the U.S.

Filming another series means that they've been at work since the early spring. And in all likelihood, they'll be touring somewhere this summer, quite possibly including some shows in America, to please all the new fans who've only had a chance to see them on television.

Yes, it's hard work, but it's worth every minute, since they enjoy every minute—except when they have to get up early (especially Bradley)! The more they work together and get to know each other, the better they get at what they do. And by now they've also recorded a second album, which will be finding its way into stores soon, keeping them very much in the public eye and in the charts, which is exactly where they deserve to be with their very catchy pop music. Even if they don't write the songs themselves (and most pop artists don't write their own material), they sing them so well and so appealingly that it's impossible to resist what they do. They've put it all together in a pretty incredible way.

So is it all a dream come true? You bet. A chance to sing and dance and have a good laugh with some mates *and* get paid for it? Life really doesn't get any better than that. And when the records you make soar straight into the charts, well, then you know you're doing something right. When their album was finally released in Britain in October 1999, it entered the charts at number two, which isn't bad going at all.

They've been a massive success at everything they've tried, and that has nothing to do with who manages them. It's all down to the appeal they put across, the naturalism of it all, and their talent and charm. No one's going to deny that each of the boys is hunky in his own way, and the girls are pretty enough to keep the boys who watch more than happy. A little bit—okay, a *lot*—of magic is what they've got, and it works so well that you really can't say no to S Club 7. But you don't want to, either. It's an S Club thing, and everyone understands it, even the parents, who might not say much, but who still secretly watch it. But that's what an S Club party is all about. It includes *everyone*. Young, old, in between, they're all welcome. No hassle at the door, just come on in and do your thing. You'll be very glad you showed up—and you won't want to leave.

PART ONE

MEET THE CLUB

YOU KNOW by now that each member of S Club 7 is a total individual. No one's trying to be a clone of anyone else, nor would they want to be. You've got a bunch of people with very strongly developed characters here. Four girls and three guys who might possibly all have become stars on their own, but who make a team to beat the world. They're fun to be around, the kind of girls and guys who'd have you in stitches if you actually could spend a day with them. They're young enough to know what it's like to be a kid, but old enough to be willing to work all the hours of the day.

Of course, they all come from somewhere, and they all have families and backgrounds, performing, doing this and that. You never get to hear about all of that in the series (well, it *is* fiction!), so maybe it's time to do a little detective work and open the S Club files to dish about Jo, Bradley, Hannah, Jon, Tina, Paul, and Rachel.

Not a single one of them is that ordinary. And what they have in common is ambition, a desire to use the talent they were given and make the most of it. Plenty of people are born with gifts, but few actually make a real attempt to use them. In the case of this lot, the gifts were in the entertainment field. But everyone has at least one gift—in sports, academics, anywhere—that they re-

ally should use as much as they can. In that regard, S
Club 7 are perfect role models. Believe in yourself, work
hard, and you'll get there.

It's been a head-over-heels life since they were selected for the group, but not a single one of them regrets
it. It's been the best time of their lives, and from the way
things seem to be going, it could last a long time. But
even though their faces are now known by a lot of people
around the world, don't expect the Club to be pulling any
star trips on anybody. It wasn't *that* long ago that they
were all pretty much unknowns, doing what they could
to get by and looking for better roles or singing jobs. So
there's no attitude, they don't think they're any better
than you or me, and they'd be happy to sit down and
talk to you if you ever run into them in an airport or,
well . . . on a beach somewhere.

Seven people, seven lives that have come together and
made something bigger than any of them could have
imagined for themselves. It's luck, and good timing. But
it's also talent and a lot of hard work. And those, as
you'll find out, have never been in short supply among
the members of the Club. So, without too much more
ado, let's start turning the spotlight on them and see just
who they really are.

JO

JO. SHE'S the blonde with the straight hair, the loud, no-nonsense attitude, and the brilliant singing voice. She the Essex Girl of the group, and proud of it.

And what is an Essex Girl? Well, Essex, not far from London, is pretty much to England what New Jersey is to America. Rightly or wrongly, people make fun of it and the people who come from there. Where New Jersey is (wrongly) considered the home of big hair on girls, and people without a clue, so is Essex—again wrongly. But Jo takes it all in stride.

"The others are forever ribbing me about it, and in one scene they even make a joke at my expense, but I find it really funny!"

It's probably just as well that she has a sense of humor about it, since she's had to grow up with it. In fact, on the rare occasions she has a few days at home, she still has to deal with it, since she still lives with her mum and dad and her brother and sister . . . in Essex.

Jo O'Meara, to give her full name, was born on April 29, 1979, so she's twenty-one now. You'll have noticed that she has at least one tattoo (the barbed wire on her left arm), but there are in fact four more, including a dolphin on her stomach. And she has a pierced belly button.

Growing up, she wasn't very girlie. Dolls didn't interest her at all—instead you were more likely to find her playing with the toys the boys were using. All through her childhood, she was a real tomboy—and there's still some of that in her, as she shows in the television series. She's not afraid to get her hands dirty (remember, this is the girl who took the engine from Howard's car on the show, even though it wasn't really her who did it); she can always put another coat of nail polish on later!

But just because she was a tomboy and she's not afraid to say exactly what she's thinking, don't imagine that Jo is hard all the way through. Quite the opposite. Under that hard shell (which isn't very thick) there's a real softie lurking inside. This is the girl who brought her two favorite stuffed animals (Donald Duck and Gus the Gorilla) to America with her for comfort and company, and who works to support the endangered Asian elephant.

However, she's tough enough not to be a romantic. On the show, Jo was forever receiving letters from Robert, her boyfriend at home, at least until she tried to dump him (without realizing that he'd popped over to visit, and was standing right behind her). The real Jo would react exactly the same way. Love letters and poetry have absolutely no effect on her; if anything, she finds all the mushy stuff to be a real turnoff. Lovey-dovey simply isn't in her book. So you can strike the shy, sensitive types as possible boyfriends. But also all the muscled hunks she saw on the Florida beaches. They didn't do a thing for her, either.

But it's not about just pulling the blokes, although that's a lot of fun. It's about Jo doing what she does. The Club stay too busy—and are too much on the move—for any of that. And long-distance love just doesn't really cut it for Jo. Which makes the fact that she actually does have a boyfriend at home a bit tough. But so far they've managed very well.

Her big thing is singing, and it always has been, ever since she first realized she had a good voice. That came about when she was twelve, thanks to a karaoke machine. The family was messing about, with her dad doing his best Frank Sinatra (which is evidently pretty good). Jo decided to give it a try, and everyone, including her, was pretty impressed by the results. Her father suggested she stick with the singing, and she did. After that she sang in a couple of bands with friends, but as soon as she was fifteen, she left school (in Britain, it's perfectly legal to quit school at fifteen). At that point, she became a professional singer, making her living on the club circuit, entertaining people in restaurants and pubs, and then eventually finding a regular gig. What's surprising, though, is the *type* of singing Jo did before joining the Club. She was making a living as a singer in a country-themed restaurant in Kent, outside London. She'd be there every night belting out the latest Young Country hits from America for the guests, getting home about one A.M., feeling pretty shattered.

The thing is, Jo loves country music, all of it, the old and the new. It's something that just hits her where she lives. So you'd think that being in the U.S., especially in Florida, she'd be going crazy, hitting every place she could to listen to country. Not so. If she did that, the others would have given her such a bad time that her life would have been a misery. Instead she just stocked up on CDs and listened in private. And just because she's into country, that doesn't mean she dressed the part, other than when she was at work. You'd be unlikely to find her in a skirt and petticoats, all decked out for line dancing. She owns a pair of boots, but the only time she'd ever wear them was for work, where it was pretty much a uniform. And they certainly weren't in her luggage when she traveled to the States.

Jo might not be much of a girlie, but there's one area where she makes no attempt to hide her gender, and that's when it comes to shopping. Being close to Miami was pretty much like being in paradise for her and all the other girls in the band. Give them a free day and they were off to hit the shops of South Beach, or the Galleria Mall (where some of the show was filmed).

"Me, Rachel, and Hannah went on a right shopping spree and spent over $300 in under an hour. Then my dad phoned me up and said, 'I hope you haven't been spending loads of money!' and I was like 'Of course not, Dad,' when I had all these bags in my hands!"

The shopping was brilliant, and the weather beat England without a contest, but there were things about home that Jo missed while she was gone for the extended period of the filming. The main one was tea bags. Ask any Brit, and they'll tell you that you can't get a decent cup of tea in America, even in Florida, which caters to British tourists. So Jo did the obvious thing, and brought her own tea bags with her. Even then it didn't work. Not because she can't make a cup of tea, she'd be quick to insist, but because the water was different, or some similar reason. Well, of *course*.

The Jo we all see on television in the series is a bit more over the top than the Jo in real life. To just hear her chatting, she's still bright and perky, but a bit more low-key—a testament to her acting abilities (which she didn't even know she had). But she's still one to make the barbed comments and take the wind out of other people's sails if they get a bit above themselves. She's real, very real. She's even willing to admit that, just like the lads, she burps in public. It might not exactly be ladylike, but, as she says, "Everyone does it, don't they?"

It was pure luck that Jo even auditioned for this gig. She was at the restaurant, singing country, when a couple of executives from 19 Management came in to eat. One of them was impressed and suggested she try out for a new project that would involve both recording and television. Jo turned in a demo tape of her singing, as well as attending the audition, but she never expected to be chosen for S Club 7, since she didn't think her abilities really fit the bill. She sang country, wasn't an actress, and didn't think she'd done too brill in the audition. Then, when she didn't hear anything for a long time, she assumed it had all come to nothing. So she was surprised to get home from work about one o'clock in the morning to be told by her father that there'd been message saying she was in—and that she'd be leaving for Italy in a couple of days! To call it a shock was something of an understatement. She was running round the house screaming with joy! Her main concern was whether she'd be able to get along with the other members, but from the moment they met, that wasn't a worry, Everyone was outgoing and excited (although probably none more than Jo).

If you want to get on Jo's good side, here are a few tips that will help you. Don't speak to her first thing in the morning, because she's always grumpy after she wakes up. It takes her a little while (and a strong cup of tea) to really get with the program every day. And don't comment on her habit of picking mascara off her eyelashes. She knows she does it, and she's trying to stop. You might also try buying her onion rings (she loves 'em!), or take her to a store that sells perfume—buying perfume just happens to be her weakness—in other words, she always smells good. Her other favorite occupation is keeping Bradley in line (well, someone has to, and Jo took it upon herself), so you could try being Bradley and bratty for a day if you wanted to make her happy. Of course, you might just end up living to regret it, too. Actually, she and Bradley are great mates—they became firm friends the day they met at the airport on their way to Italy, and have remained so ever since. But she does keep her eye on him to make sure he doesn't cheat on any of his girlfriends.

At twenty-one, it wouldn't be too astonishing if Jo had her own place instead of living with her family. After all, the others, even the younger ones, have their own flats. But Jo is really close to her brother, sister, and parents.

So much so, she said, that if the world was ending, "I'd order Chinese with all my family and talk about how great our lives had been."

She's incredibly happy and fulfilled being a member of the S Club, getting to sing and travel all the time. But the place she was really looking forward to visiting was New Zealand. Why? Because the Club are big there (they are, by the way)? No, something that goes back, as always with her, to family: "I've got a lot of family out there who I haven't seen for years."

There's no "leader" in this band, but Jo, simply by the size of her personality, can dominate the others (they might also say the size of her voice, but don't believe it for a minute). Certainly, though, when it comes to singing, she's one who does take the lead, since she was the only one making her living at that before the show.

And that wasn't just singing country in the restaurant. She'd actually been in a recording studio before, and had a record out. It had never been seen or heard in England, except in Jo's house, but in Germany it had been a top twenty hit, which meant that she came into the project with some very solid experience that would be useful.

On stage she's perfectly comfortable, but then again she should be. This sort of thing has been her living for a while. The Club have played a number of gigs, all over Britain, everything from entertaining the senior managers for Woolworth's (!) to radio station roadshows, or the one that Jo loved above all, Party In The Park. Since it was for charity, there was a great atmosphere, but it was more people than they'd ever sung to in their lives—one hundred thousand folks all over London's Hyde Park. The only way most of them could see the band (whose "Bring It All Back" was on *Top of the Pops*) was through the giant video screens behind the stage. For Jo, it was all nerve-wracking—at least until the music began. Then it was a blur of sound and movement for the next three minutes, until they left the stage and almost collapsed in their dressing area. The energy and the buzz, she said, had been unlike anything she'd experienced before. It was a very definite high point in her career with the Club.

But it's all been a series of high points, really, and there are more and more of them. Jo loved Florida and Los Angeles (which is probably just as well, since she's spending a lot of time on the West Coast filming the show's second season). It's all been new and it's all been good. She thought she was a professional before all this happened, but with working so much, she's learned what professionalism is all about. And it means being able to get up early. *Very* early. Often in Florida, they had to be up and about at six in the morning, sometimes even earlier, and once, when they were taping *Back to the Fifties* in LA, they got their wake up call at two-thirty A.M.! Sleep has become a luxury for them all, and they've learned to take it when they can, even if it's just a ten-minute nap. Add on to that all the traveling and the jet lag, and you've got a bunch of people who'd sometimes rather spend a free night sleeping than clubbing! So when Jo has a free day, her morning tends to be the middle of the afternoon!

She understands full well how lucky she is. Not just to be a part of a band that's having hits and worldwide success, but to be working with a bunch of people she genuinely likes. It doesn't get any better than this, and she knows it.

One thing Jo has never done is follow the crowd. If that had been the case, she'd never have ended up as a singer. She wouldn't have had her belly button pierced, or undergone the tattoos. And it's that spirit of adventure that makes every day with the Club an absolute joy for her. She loves not knowing exactly what she'll be doing tomorrow, and always having to be on her toes—quite literally at times when she's dancing.

There's a special bloke in Jo's life, but the way things are going, it's unlikely there will be wedding bells for a while. She's simply on the move too much, hopping between continents all the time. And even when she's in

England, there's recording to do, shows to play, or just simply to catch up on sleep and chill with her family. It's why the other members of the Club are so important. They're good friends who are going through the same thing. From the very first, they've socialized even when they weren't working—it's like having another family. But dating one of the guys in the band would be a disaster, and everyone knows it. So they keep it all strictly platonic.

The other thing is now that Jo's a star, there are going to be people after her simply because she *is* famous. But her feet are firmly enough planted on the ground to deal with that. No problem. She has her priorities straight, and the top two will always be her family and her career. She's going to have a great time running with this for as long as it lasts (and that could well be years), and then quite probably meet someone and settle down to raise her own family. And don't be too surprised if that ends up being in Essex. You can take the girl out of Essex, but you can never completely take the Essex out of the girl!

Florida, LA . . . it's all amazing, and Jo is still trying to get her head around it. To wake up, go outside and have miles of ocean right there, sandy beaches and sunshine. It's what people dream about, and it's the kind of life she's been living. Even if she has to work hard, it's worthwhile. This gives her real pleasure, and it would even if it hadn't made her into a star. How many people from England have the chance to take an afternoon off and go shopping in South Beach . . . even though she sometimes says that shopping bores her (yeah, right!). What a load of parp.

While she can be the outgoing one, at times Jo does like to be quiet and reflective, as we all do. And much to her amazement, in Miami she became the butt of an ongoing practical joke. Every night Jon and Brad would scratch on the door of her room, just loud enough for her to hear. And every day Jo would say how the noises scared her. When the truth came out, you could say she wasn't best pleased with a couple of lads.

Overall, though, she'd do anything for her friends. If they were broke and she had a little money, she'd give it to them without a second thought—she's the generous type.

And that, then, is Jo. She's a complex kind of girl, always up for a laugh, but equally ready to get down and work hard for as long as it takes to get it right. You couldn't ask for a better mate, but you'd better be prepared to be able to take a joke. Oh yeah, and she can sing a bit, too. But if you're in the Club, you'd better be ready for anything—just like Jo is!

PAUL

PAUL IS the cool one with the really short hair, the one who tends to dress in sleeveless shirts to show off his hunky arms. He looks a bit moody and hard at times, but he's not really. Well, he does like being quiet from time to time (on journeys, he's the one who's likely to vanish into his headphones and spend the entire trip just listening to music).

Paul Cattermole (which, you have to admit, isn't your usual showbiz kind of name) was born on March 7, 1977, making him twenty-three years old. Apart from just plain Paul, the others call him Cattermole, Guacamole, or Gwaks. He's the brain of the band, as it were—not that any of them are dumb—the kid who actually liked physics at school, perhaps because his grandfather was a particle physicist—it's in the blood. Then again, music is also in his genes. Paul's great-grandfather was one of the first managers of the legendary Abbey Road recording studios in London, where the Beatles, among many others, made their records. With all that going for him, how could he have been anything but a Club member?

Well, except for a trick of fate, Paul might never have got into entertainment. For a long time, he had two big ambitions in school. The first was to follow in the family footsteps and become a physicist, which would have meant years at university. The other was to become a rugby player (you've seen Paul on television, and he definitely has the build for it). It's a long way from there to singing for his supper, and a lot happened in between.

Essentially, you can place the blame on Leonard Bernstein's musical, *West Side Story*. For some reason, at the start of his teens, Paul decided to audition for a local production of the show, and won a role. Immediately he was starstruck. At that point it was a case of forget physics, forget rugby, he'd found what he wanted to do with his life. To their eternal credit, his parents encouraged him, and he joined the National Youth Music Theatre, where he took part in a production of *Pendragon*, and that completely sealed it. He was totally hooked. The play, which was about the legend of King Arthur, proved tremendously successful. So successful, in fact, that it went on tour, with Paul as a member of the touring company. After England they hit Asia, which was a great culture shock, then ended up in New York, where the play was staged at City Center Theater. And if you think that wasn't a major buzz for Paul, then you'd be greatly mistaken.

Never mind university any more. Paul had his heart set on drama school, and that was exactly what he did, attending Mountview Drama School for a few years to learn all the techniques of acting.

But there was another passion he'd developed while he was a teenager, and that was music. He loved it, and still does. While he was at Mountview, in the evenings he began singing with a band, and had a really good voice. To be fair, it helped him as an actor (someone who can also sing can go after more jobs), but mostly he was doing it out of love of music. It was, however, vastly different from S Club, since, he said, the music leaned more toward punk rock, a little like the Red Hot Chili Peppers.

After drama school, of course, came a short course in reality. There were a lot of actors out there auditioning for a few roles, so Paul found himself doing all manner of things. They were all temporary, of course, like the job collecting garbage. But that's the way it often goes in show business; the times you spend "resting" are often longer than the times you spend working. You just stick with it because it's something you *have* to do—it comes from inside, and it's worth every kind of hardship to continue doing it.

And, of course, there's always the chance you'll become a star. Granted, it's a small chance, but even that is better than none.

When Paul found out about the auditions for S Club, he knew the same as everyone else. It would be for a band, and there'd also be a television show. Combining music and acting, his two loves, seemed ideal to him, so naturally he went. He knew he'd simply be one of many, and he had no idea of the time frame. So he auditioned, and then heard nothing. And nothing, until he'd more or less given up on it, and was auditioning for other roles. But finally, months after he'd tested, he heard that he had the part.

Now that was brilliant. Paul wasn't the type to go screaming around the apartment (known in Britain as a flat) he shared with his best friend, but he was overjoyed. If everything worked out with this, he'd be doing exactly what he wanted to do, and not scrambling for money anymore.

His first meeting with the other people who'd been selected was at Heathrow airport, when they got together to fly to Italy, where they'd rehearse and get to know each other. He was surprised, and very pleased, to see an old friend in the group. Paul and Hannah had become mates back when they were both working with the National Youth Music Theatre—in fact, they'd met on the production of *Pendragon*. Although they didn't see each other often, it was still good to know there'd be one familiar face in the crowd.

As it happened, he didn't need to worry. Everyone got

along famously. As the oldest of the guys, Paul became something of a leader for the three, although after a while, that seemed to change.

Now Paul is just Paul, one of the Club, who's just as much up for a laugh as the others, but equally ready to take it all seriously when necessary.

Amazingly, the thing he worries about most is how he looks. He likes his earlobes, but thinks his bum is way too big. Hmmm. . . . And when the Club first arrived in Florida, he was very self-conscious about his build.

"I'm just a fat little porker who ate too many pies compared to the ultrafit guys on the beach. When I first saw their physiques I was *completely* blown out of the water!"

So when he was asked to shed his top for some beach scenes, Paul was very hesitant. However, the director promised that if he wasn't happy, they'd cut them. In the end, good little trouper that he is, Paul went through with it.

He went though with something else in Miami, too—he got his left nipple pierced, to add to the piercing on his ear (it has been rumored that he has a pierced eyebrow, but if so, it's never been visible on the show or in any interview).

You might be surprised to learn that in general terms, Paul isn't exactly a hit with the girls—and that's not just the girls in the Club, to whom he's like a brother, but in general terms. By his own admission, he wouldn't even give himself "one out of ten on the romance scale." Given that he's a total cutie (that's either "love puff" or "cutesickle" in Club-speak), it all seems pretty amazing. Then again, like the others, there's no time for Paul to have a romance these days. They're simply too busy. He thinks in Club time now, not days and weeks. It's all marked by what he's scheduled to do.

And he loves every second of what he's doing. This is what he's trained for, really, bringing all the facets of his talents together. He might not have been a dancer before joining the Club, but he's learned very quickly, and no one is doubting his abilities as a singer.

Like the others, he has his favorite musical moments and gigs with the band. For him, the very top time had to be when they played the Odeon in Leicester Square, London. It was to celebrate the premiere of *Back to the Fifties*, and they were scheduled to do a show in the theater. For their dramatic entrance, they rose up to the stage in a lift, from what had originally been the organ pit. It worked beautifully, with them standing still, and out of nowhere silhouetted against the backdrop, and for Paul it will live in his memory forever.

Dancing is a natural activity for Paul. Not only does he like to go out clubbing, but he always enjoyed PE at school (PE and physics—definitely a strange kid!). He's also a major soccer fan, and is quite devoted to his favorite team, Arsenal, based in North London, and one of the top clubs in the English Premier League.

But far more than soccer, he loves his food. Give him one of those small portions that many restaurants dish up, and he's not going to be a happy camper.

"I'm sure anyone who watches *S Club 7 in Miami* will think that all I do is eat and, um, I suppose they'd be right! I'm really not fussy, I'll eat *anything*." Which might be why he worries about his bum being too big, of course. But we all know it's not. And he's not a porker, either, in spite of the way he worries. Eating out is one thing. There he can get whatever he wants. But if you were to go to Paul's for a meal, you'd probably only end up eating poached eggs—cooking is not one of his specialties. If it's a party, however, you might want to stick around, especially if you like your music loud. In fact, the worst trouble he ever got into came "when I had a party at our house with a huge sound system in the garage and the police came round at four A.M. and forced us to turn it down."

At work, Paul's a real pro—well, he does have quite a few years of experience behind him—but that doesn't mean he's always quiet on the set. Instead, like Bradley, he tends to be a bit of a prankster, winding the others up mercilessly. But when it's time for a scene, he's there, on his mark, lines all ready, although he and the others will sometimes talk to the director and change a few lines here and there. The Club do have input on the show, rather than always sticking to the script word for word. And that's how their personalities really come across.

Success really hasn't changed Paul one bit. He's still the same bloke he always was, although he does have rather more money to spend on CDs than he used to have. And music remains his top love. Get him on a plane or a train or in a limo being driven around, and it's on with the headphones. It gives him a chance to disappear from the world for a while and to enjoy a bit of quiet time, something he really doesn't get too much otherwise. All the traveling is great, and Paul loves seeing the world in a way he'd never imagined himself doing, but he still needs time to himself to chill a little, and about the only times that's possible is when they're actually moving. It's not always the most satisfactory way, but you take what you can get.

His previous experience, and his time in drama school, has stood Paul in good stead for all the rigor and discipline of working with the Club. He's used to being ready and being up, even though it still took him a little time to adjust to the crazy schedules they have to keep. However, you really wouldn't want to peek into his hotel room. Other than acting, Paul could almost have gone to school to study untidiness. Give him five minutes, and he can make his room look like it's been lived in for a week, clothes everywhere . . . including the several pairs of mustard-colored boxers he always packs.

Amazingly, considering the way he keeps his room, Paul is actually the organizer of the group, the sort of daddy to them all, keeping everyone in line (yeah, like that's going to happen . . .). And knowing who's supposed to be where and when. So there are two very different sides to his personality, which meet when you sit down and talk to him—he can be very laid-back and thoughtful.

The manic music lover, and lover of volume and excess, comes out when talking about his dream car. He'd love to own an old Cobra, the American sports car with a roaring, revving engine, although how he'd ever get to really drive it on English roads is another question entirely. He doesn't actually own a car at the moment. He had one, an old Mini, but he basically drove it until it fell apart, and since then there hasn't been the time to replace it. He loves to drive, but these days it's more a case of the band being driven everywhere. Which is good, in a way, since it does give Paul that little bit of time to chill.

America has been an absolute blast for him (although, of course, he'd seen New York when he was younger), or at least it has been since he stopped being intimidated by the beach hunks. He loved Florida, although, unlike the girls, he didn't hare off to South Beach to go shopping at every opportunity. San Francisco was amazing, and Los Angeles—at least what he saw of it when he wasn't working—was like the American dream come to life, wide streets, palm trees, and beautiful girls—although, to his annoyance, none of them seemed that interested in him—just his luck!

Like Jo, and the rest of the band, Paul has a strong interest in animals. In his case, it's preserving the endangered black rhino. But S Club 7 as a band are strong supporters of the World Wildlife Fund, and they made a charity appearance in the fall of 1999 at Whipsnade Zoo in England to help publicize the fun and whip up some support for their cause.

It's one cause the band have put their weight and their name behind, and a very good one. But the other is equally serious—a campaign to stop bullying in schools in England. As everyone knows, it's a problem everywhere, and one that always needs to be tackled head-on.

That makes it refreshing that the Club, whose main audience is kids who go to school, are involving themselves in a movement to stamp out bullying. As anyone who's ever been bullied can tell you, there's nothing humorous about it.

But they all have their hearts in the right place. They make their living entertaining people, but all of them are determined to give something back. They've been lucky, apart from being talented, and they realize it.

So for now, Paul is just grooving on being a part of the Club, even if they tease him about having smelly feet (which he claims is a total lie!). It's a great life being part of the 7, and it's exactly what he would have picked if he'd had his choice. Maybe it all gets a bit mad at times, but the good times far outweigh anything bad. Sooner or later he'll come across a girl who fancies him, and then there'll be romance in the air for Paul. But probably not immediately, given the schedule he keeps.

Paul is one of the Club members with real acting experience (along with Jon and Hannah), and that balances with the singers (Jo and Bradley) and the dancers (Rachel and Tina), so that they can all help each other with different skills. Like the others, he's committed to the Club. It's his big break, it's made him known, a star, and he's very grateful for that. It still amazes him when he's stopped for autographs. In time, though, it wouldn't be too surprising to see him try for the occasional dramatic role. For now, there's simply no time. The members of the club are too busy to consider anything else (and that's a good thing, really). Between hitting the charts and a top television show, time off has become something Paul's heard about but rarely experiences, and that's the type of situation most actors would love to be in.

He may not get the girls, but he has his mates in the Club, and they all look out for each other. This is great fun, a dream job for any young performer, with the kind of international exposure that goes beyond amazing. Sand, surf, singing . . . who wouldn't be jealous of Paul?

And, in reality, he probably doesn't have to worry too much as to whether he's fanciable. The girls might not be surrounding him, but it's probably only because he's been moving so fast that they haven't been able to catch up yet!

HANNAH

HANNAH'S THE one with the hair that changes all the time, from straight, to sort-of dreadlocks (it was actually done by some very thick gel, and washed out a few days later). She's also the tiny one, as so many jokes in the script of the television show have pointed out.

Hannah Spearritt looks sweet and angelic, as if she'd never even consider doing anything wrong. But, as she pointed out, "I'm actually a mad party animal—probably the worst of all of us! I've got a lot of go in me, believe me!"

She's also the cute one, probably because she's the youngest (okay, Bradley is the same age, but Hannah is definitely *cuter* than Bradley). But behind all that is a lot of professional experience. In fact, Hannah has been in show business longer than any other member of the Club—since she was three years old, in fact.

Hannah was born on April 1, 1981, and raised in a town called Great Yarmouth, on the east coast of England. It's a fishing port, but also a big vacation resort, with a long beach, and plenty of water (so she was no stranger to surf and sand when she got to Miami, although Florida was a bit warmer than where she was from). From the time she was born she was a gorgeous child, and it was her looks that got Hannah her first job—

modeling in a Mothercare catalogue when she was three. Mothercare is a British chain that sells maternity gear, as well as clothes and other things for babies and young children (modeling for Mothercare was one of the first jobs that Emma B. from the Spice Girls had, by the way).

That got her started on the idea of performing, although it was just an idea at that point, and she began going to dance school once a week. When she started real school, however, it was athletics that took over, and she emerged as a talented runner and tennis player, so much that she dreamed of becoming a professional athlete.

So what happened? Well, you could blame it all on *Annie*. When Hannah was twelve, she auditioned for a production of the musical and won a part. It was her first real exposure to theater, and she loved it so much that then and there she said to herself, "Yeah, I want to perform." Now, saying that was one thing, but making it happen was altogether different. Some people have all the desire in the world, but just aren't quite good enough. That wasn't the case with Hannah. As soon as *Annie* was over, she took part in nationwide auditions for the National Youth Music Theatre, and was accepted—so she was in there with Paul.

Her first real part was in *Pendragon*, alongside Paul, and like him, she traveled all over with the show, even the New York dates. The National Youth Music Theatre wasn't a school, though, it was strictly an extracurricular activity. Hannah didn't go to any theatrical school. Instead, it was just regular school for her, including school plays and choirs (which was where she got her singing experience) with a lot of extra drama work on top of it all. Her final production with the NYMT ended up in the West End of London (England's equivalent of Broadway in New York).

At the age of sixteen she left school to concentrate on her acting, and to try and make a living at it. She auditioned for the British teen soap, *Grange Hill*, but didn't get the part. For her age, she had a good resume under her belt, which helped, but it was still scary. As well as live theater, she also wanted to break into television, and that came about through one of the British staples—a costume drama. In *The Cater Street Hangman*, set in Victorian times, she played a maid (one of the British teen mags dug up a picture of her dressed for the role and printed it, which caused her a lot of embarrassment), and then she found work on a show called *Bugsy Malone*. They were small parts, but everyone has to start somewhere. *Blue Peter*, a very long-running children's magazine show, had her on in what might just have been the most challenging role she'll ever undertake—Hannah had to lie in the rain for three hours without moving. And for anyone who knows hyper Hannah, that *had* to be a major challenge for her. But it was work, and that was the name of the game. Unlike Paul, Hannah had decided not to go to drama school, but to try straight off to make it on her own talent. That meant every job was important, even the gig on that televised National Lottery, which had proved to be a launching pad for new young stars. In Hannah's case, it led to work on commercials, most specifically a commercial for Mercedes, which aired not only in Britain, but also in the U.S. for about a year.

After that she heard about the audition for S Club 7 and went to that. She could act, she could sing, she knew a bit about dancing. But, like Jo, it was a long time before she heard that she was in, and then she just had a couple of days to get everything together and catch the plane to Italy with the others to begin work. It was a happy shock to meet Paul, to find there was someone she knew in the group.

Then again, Hannah is so outgoing that it wouldn't have mattered if they'd all been complete strangers. She'd soon have known them well, anyway. This is the kind of girl who makes a hobby out of talking to complete strangers on planes. She loves it because you can say just about anything and everything, safe in the knowledge that you'll never ever see them again.

Hannah might be all grown up, but she does have one habit that goes back to childhood. She still sleeps with her teddy bear (if you look closely, you can see him in bed with her in some episodes of the show). His name is Little Ted, and she's always taken him everywhere, making him an extremely well-traveled stuffed animal! But no more than Hannah herself, which suits her down to the ground (as it were) since she simply *loves* to travel. If she weren't in the Club, traveling would be what she'd be doing when she wasn't working. So things have ended up perfectly for her—she gets the very best of both worlds (and she gets to travel in style). She'd already seen New York before, but she was just a kid then; it was a different matter when the Club finally hit the Big Apple. But her very favorite place was San Francisco, even though they were only there for two days doing promotion for the show, and she didn't have much opportunity to see the place. It's on her list of places to visit again.

While she throughly enjoys being on the move, it's been hard for her to be away from home so much. She remains very close to her parents, although she doesn't get to see them often. In fact, before leaving for Miami to film, she hadn't seen her folks for a few weeks, and there was no chance to get home for a visit before flying out, since they were so busy. So, as soon as the plane landed at Heathrow, her first order of business was to dash back to Great Yarmouth to see them, to be pampered, and to catch up on everything.

One thing everyone notices about Hannah is that she's *always* smiling. It's to the point where you have to wonder if she's ever down.

"No, never!" she said. "I'm a pretty happy person all the time!"

Well, almost all the time. The tedium of filming all day, every day did get to her, and to each of the others, from time to time. That's only natural, however, since it involves a lot of sitting around and waiting, which isn't one of Hannah's best qualities. Once she gets going, though, she's happy as a lark, and all of them do everything they can to make each minute fun, playing tricks on each other and just having as many laughs as they can pack into a day.

Romance doesn't figure heavily into Hannah's current plans. She did have a serious boyfriend—a surfer who lived in Cornwall, England, where there are plenty of waves—but he's been an ex for quite a while now. He was the only boy she's ever been "mushy" over. Since then she's dated people, but after about a week she's tended to get bored with them, and moved on. Since joining the Club, there simply hasn't been time. While she definitely fancied the lifeguard she had to chat up on the show, there was no chance to get to know him, and the Florida beach boys didn't really do much for her, other than remind her of her ex.

She did see plenty of talent when all the girls went out clubbing in Miami, but with a very full schedule, there was no real opportunity to do anything about it. No sooner would she have gotten to know someone than it would be time to move somewhere else. And she didn't even get any snogging scenes in the show, although she'd have definitely enjoyed some!

Having a good time is definitely Hannah's hobby, and she's very good at it, too. She might look all sweet and innocent, but don't let that fool you. Inside is a real party animal who hates to stop while there's still a party going on. It explains why one of her favorite people is H from the British band Steps, whose debut was released here earlier this year. "We all like him 'cause he's always in a party mood," she said, which explains a lot. But a party can be anything. It doesn't have to be clubbing and dancing or loud music. Hannah can make a party out of shopping, and she did on one occasion when she, Jo, and Rachel went into Miami and managed to blow quite a bit of money in just an hour. Did she feel guilty? Not really.

She'd worked so hard that she'd earned a little break, and every girl knows that new clothes make you feel good.

Something else that makes her feel good is pizza, which is one reason she loved being in America. No matter what anyone might claim, pizza in England just isn't the same. Perhaps that's because, until about twenty-five years ago, no one over there had ever heard of it! Whatever the reason, Hannah just fell in love with pizza in the States. But only if it was a pizza with everything— and she means *every* thing—on it. The higher it was piled, the better. She couldn't tuck all of it away, of course, since she's small, and unlike Jo, remains bit ladylike, but she could do her share of damage to it. And the leftovers were always good for breakfast the next day.

Actually, for all that she loves to party, Hannah does have a reflective side. Give her free time on the set during a day of shooting, and she'll settle down with a book (which meant that she read quite a lot in Florida, since there was more waiting than shooting). But at the same time, give her a few minutes when there are going to be no demands on her, and she'll settle down to sleep. Like the others, Hannah has found sleep to be a luxury; there simply isn't enough time for it (which might well be why she'd love to have an extra day in the week "so I'd have more time to do things"). She's learned to sleep almost anywhere, and to live off little catnaps. If there's ten minutes before she's due in makeup, she'll curl up on the floor and be off in a second.

And everywhere she goes, Hannah carries her camera. She records just about everything, all the cities the Club visits, the things she does, the people she sees. It's her way of being able to bring back memories of everything, although she does go through an awful lot of film! But it's worthwhile, because all the places, and a lot of the faces, have some kind of meaning for her—and a picture can be worth a thousand words.

Although she does like to get dressed up—at least at

times—Hannah is most comfortable in some kind of tank top and something casual, with sandals or trainers on her feet. None of this high-heel parp for her, thank you very much! It's a reflection of the down-to-earth personality she has. And one item she'd never be caught dead in is "a flowery dress." No little miss here, then.

The way Hannah really is, that's what comes across on *S Club 7 in Miami*. Bubbly, very cute, but with a bit of a temper at times—well, she is a redhead, after all—and short. The others make jokes about it. There have been jokes in the script, and she's even been asked to stand on a box. But she's much happier being short; she has no desire to be a six-foot-tall Amazon. Why? Because "small people can definitely get away with a lot more!" And she should know. Of course, being a titch can have a downside, too. She's the one who's always being lifted up and hoisted over someone's shoulder!

For someone who never trained as a singer or a dancer, Hannah's shown that she has a natural talent at both. But it's acting where she really shines. When you watch the show, just study her. It's her real love (apart from athletics), and she's very, very good at it. It's subtle, exaggerating different aspects of who she is to give an impression, and she does it excellently. While the Hannah on the show is mostly her, it's not a complete representation, although you come away thinking it is. To create that illusion is the real acting talent. It's pretty much certain that at some point in the future, Hannah will go after lots of dramatic roles, and probably surprise people who just think of her as a pop star. She didn't get into acting for the money—most actors rarely make money, anyway—but because she loves acting and the feeling she gets from being onstage.

Back in England, Hannah shares a flat in London with a good friend (at least, she thinks she does—it's not too often that she sees it anymore). From the time she turned sixteen and became a professional actress, that's been where she needed to be, where the work was. And, of course, it's where all the best clubs and parties are, which makes for a major bonus.

It's been quite a long road for Hannah to reach the Club, and she's put in a lot of work along the way, paying her dues, and knowing what it's like to be unemployed as well as working. All of which means she really values what she's doing now. Not just because it's a job, but because it's about the best acting job ever. There's travel, tons of fun, a chance to sing and dance, and on top of it all, she's acquired six new best friends. Can life get any better than that? Well, no, it can't . . . and that's why Hannah's glad to be a member of the Club.

JON

JON IS the real baby of the bunch, the little blond cutie with the flyaway hair and the serious manner. He really *is* the baby of the crew, a year younger than Hannah, and almost a year younger than Bradley. For all that, however, he probably has the biggest professional resume behind him of any member of the Club.

Jon (he has no middle name) Lee was born on April 26, 1982, just outside London. Not long after, his family moved down to Devon, in the west of England. It's a pretty, rural area, but there's generally not a lot to do there.

Somehow or other, Jon must have had acting in his blood. His love for it seemed to come out of nowhere, but from the beginning, in school plays, his talent was quite evident. The problem was, living in Devon, there wasn't a whole lot of opportunity for him to act, other than amateur dramatics, and his ability went well beyond that. He began auditioning for professional roles in London (which was quite a trek—a good three hours each way on the train!), and when he got his first part, the Lee family made a move back to London.

Then again, it was quite a part he'd won.

He'd been picked to play Oliver in a revival of *Oliver!*, the musical based on Charles Dickens's *Oliver*

Twist. Back in the sixties, the show had been incredibly successful as both a stage musical and a film. A lot of famous people had gone through the cast, including, back in the day, Phil Collins as a teenager playing the Artful Dodger. It was going to be a big, glitzy production, and it would be staged at one of the world's best-known theaters, the London Palladium.

That guaranteed him a lot of exposure, and the show ran for quite a long time before finally closing. For Jon, it was about the best experience he could hope for. Not only did he learn what it was like to be a star, but also what it took to really become a professional. With eight shows a week, his life consisted of school and work, with precious little time for fun, or even for family. But this was what he'd wanted to do, and he stuck with it. He loved to act, and since *Oliver!* was a musical, there was also plenty of opportunity to sing.

When the show was over, however, there was the question of what he'd do next. It was never a case of thinking that was all. There was always something else to go after, and in Jon's case, he wanted to make the move to television. Of course, so did most actors. It meant an awful lot of people would see you. In Britain, week after week the highest-rated shows are the soap operas, which air in the evening, rather than in the daytime like in America. The two top soaps, which consistently duke it out for the number one slot, are *Coronation Street* and *EastEnders*, which appear on rival networks. *Coronation Street* is set in a fictional northern town, just outside Manchester, while *EastEnders* is supposed to take place in the East End of London, so there's a North-South divide between the two, as well.

A new character was being created on *EastEnders*, a young man named Josh, and auditions were being held for the role. Alerted by his agent, Jon went along—and walked away with the part! It was the type of role to make every young male actor sit up and pay attention—not just a one-off appearance, but recurring, with the possibility of being a continual character. That meant regular work, possibly long-term steady work, and also recognition and fans.

Certainly, Jon was happy to be playing Josh, but more for the challenge than the material gain. He was still young, only fourteen, and there were plenty of other things on his mind, the topmost of which had to be school. If Josh really did become a regular on the show, it would be great, but if not his world wasn't about to come crashing down. The professional habits he'd learned on the stage served him well in television. With three episodes a week, work was continuous, and he had to be ready and, wherever possible, get his lines right the first time.

Luckily for Jon (and for everyone else) he had—and still has—a photographic memory for lines, which made learning his speeches easy, and saying them almost as easy, although, like every actor, he would blow it from time to time (and still does occasionally, by the way). But he was always on time and prepared for his speeches, without any of the temperament some stars might show here and there.

In the end, Josh didn't become a regular character on the show, and was phased out. By then, Jon was sixteen. He'd finished school, and was now a professional actor in every sense of the word. He heard about the audition for S Club, knowing nothing more than it was for a group, and would involve music and a television show. At the time he was auditioning for lots of things, although this was probably the biggest of all. But time went by, he heard nothing, and had almost forgotten about it by the time he got the phone call saying he was in, and that a ticket was waiting for him to fly to Italy. Luckily, none of his other auditions had turned up trumps, so he was perfectly free to meet the others and get started in the Club. For all his professional experience, and the auditions he'd attended, he didn't know any of the others— but they didn't remain strangers for very long!

While all the others have pictures of their families to remind them of home, Jon has something a little bit different by his bed—a photograph of his dog. Molly, the canine, is five and is Jon's very special love.

"I absolutely *adore* that dog and miss her to bits when I'm away from home," he said. "She thinks she's a human being . . ." which probably explains why she spends a lot of time watching television, her favorite program being one called *Pet Rescue*—honest! Like the others, Jon phoned home regularly when he was in Florida (and they all check in with home when they're on the road), but in his case it was often to make sure Molly was doing fine.

Of course, with all that love for his dog, Jon doesn't have much left over for any possible romance. On the show he leaves that to others, like Bradley and Rachel—in fact, during the entire season he only got to chat up a couple of girls! Overall, though, he didn't really mind. However, when Cameron Diaz was filming in South Beach he was seriously looking for her, although she might have been a little bit too old for him.

So no, besides Molly, there really is no girl in Jon's life. It would be unfair to both of them, with him away so much. Deffo not the best way to carry on a relationship. If he ever spends more than a couple of weeks at home and not working, though, you can almost lay odds that the girls will be crowding around his door. After all, who can resist that face . . . or that hair?

Ah yes, the hair. As you know from the show, his 'do is Jon's pride and joy. It's changed a little from when he joined the band. Pictures of the very early days show it (gasp!) flatter and parted in the middle. Now it sticks up a bit, very carefully cut to look flyaway, which happens to suit him very well, thank you.

And it's not just on the show that Jon loves his hair; it's every bit the same in real life, which makes it so surprising that he once had his head shaved "which was a nightmare." But, obviously, it grew out again, and in a way he really likes.

He also sports a couple of tattoos, one of which can be seen on the show, an image of a sun on his left arm. But while he was in Florida, he got another one done, also on his left arm, a snake that reaches from his wrist to his elbow (ouch!), and there's no doubt the next season will be showing that one quite a bit.

Unlike some of the others, Jon isn't a very impetuous person. Perhaps because he's been working so hard and professionally for such a long time that he's become quite serious, even though it seems like a bit of a burden to carry around this lot. That much of the character he plays on the show really is him. Not that he doesn't like his fun, but work is definitely work, and not a time for just horsing around. It doesn't really matter to Jon if he comes across as a bit of a nerd, or a party pooper while all the others seem ready to get wild. He can join in anytime he likes, and he does. And certainly, in those rare moments when he's not working, he can get as crazy as anyone. Invite him to a party, and you'll see. He'll rock the house. On one occasion he didn't leave a party until "three in the afternoon the day after! I never leave until they tell me to get out!" So there's a definite party animal lurking under the serious smile after all!

One thing Jon is definitely not is egotistical. In a way, you could excuse him if he was, since the last six years have seen him do more than many people accomplish in a lifetime. But until *S Club 7 in Miami* was aired (in Britain it's shown by the BBC), he'd never watched himself on television. He couldn't stand it. The whole idea of seeing himself on the small screen just made his skin crawl. But at least he made an exception for the Club! But as an indication of how small his ego is, his favorite scenes from the series came from the very beginning, as the band flew out to Miami: "I really like those, probably because I'm not in them!" Now is that pleasant, or what?

Certainly the photographic memory of his has helped

him with the show. While the others work on their lines, Jon just glances at the script, then gets it all perfect the next day. Or usually he does. One time when they were working with the alligator (Howard's pet/watchdog), Jon did manage to blow it, but in his defense he had two really long speeches. Other than that he was word-perfect every single time, which is about as professional as anyone can hope to get, really.

So what did Jon miss about home when he spent more than two months in Miami? Well, there was Molly of course, and his family, but he was also one of those *very* weird people who missed the English weather. Now, how strange is that? He'd happily trade in sun, sand, and water for gray skies and rain any day of the week! Well, they do say it takes all sorts, although you seriously have to wonder about him. . . .

The other thing he missed was his favorite soap opera. No, not *EastEnders*, the one he appeared in, but its main rival *Coronation Street*. He's been watching it as long as he can remember, and couldn't bear not to know what was going on. So he got his parents to tape every episode—and that's four episodes a week—so he could have a marathon viewing after he got home. And you have to admit, that's some serious dedication.

So all in all, Jon is a very decent sort of bloke; he just knows how to divide his time between work and partying. He's considerate . . . he'd love to invent "a robot that tidies my room. My mum always ends up doing it and she needs a break." Well, maybe he could ask Paul, who was the physics brain, to put one together for him!

You're not likely to catch Paul getting into trouble (unlike, say, Bradley . . . well, maybe we shouldn't just pick on Bradley). You probably won't even catch him arriving somewhere late, since that's one of his pet peeves. Even though he's been almost permanently tired since joining the Club, what with their crazy schedule, he's awake as soon as they're called, and ready to roll. Like the others, he's concerned about the environ-

ment, and as part of their World Wildlife Fund involvement, he's been working to help save the orangutan,
which is on the endangered species list.

While the others have widely varying musical tastes
(Hannah, for example, spent part of 1999 groovin' to
DMX), Jon's tastes are more to the mainstream. His all-
time favorite—Celine Dion (although you have to hope
that he got to see her before she retired from the stage).
He's also the one who, in spite of his love of English
rain, adapted most quickly to America. In fact, he found
himself picking up all kinds of America phrases, such as
"Hey!" instead of "Hello." As soon as he noticed he was
doing it, he began trying to stop. After all, it didn't quite
go with that accent.

He's a sucker for a nice smile (well, what boy isn't,
come to that?), and a believer in talismans, which is probably why he takes a marble egg everywhere with him.
He was given it for luck, and there's no denying that it
certainly hasn't brought him any bad luck. All in all, he
loves what he's doing right now. After the seriousness
of two major roles, this is a lot lighter (although probably
more demanding in terms of effort and time), and it just
confirms his feeling that acting is what he should be doing. Although, if it had all fallen apart, he'd have stayed
on at school with the intention of becoming a vet. He
genuinely does love animals, which is why he's a vege-
tarian, and has an absolute hatred of the idea of cosmetics
being tested on animals or any living creature.

And that's Jon. It's impossible not to love the baby
of the band, really, especially when he's that cute, and
seems to take everything to heart so much. But even more
so when he's that talented. You have to think that in
twenty years' time Jon Lee will still be a star. Maybe not
as a singer (although who can tell?), but definitely as an
actor. It seems a near-certainty, really.

RACHEL

EVERY BAND needs a brunette girl, and in Rachel, S Club has one of the best. Not only is she an utter babe, she can also sing, dance, and act. And can you ask more than that? Well, judging by the show, you could ask that she be a little less self-centered, a little more considerate of others, and possibly slightly less of a fashion plate.

But that's television, of course, and Rachel is a character on a show. In real life, Rachel Stevens is an absolute sweetie. About the only trait she shares with *Miami*'s Rachel is the love of fashion. At least, that's what she says, "but the others think it's me down to a tee. Thanks, guys!"

Rachel Stevens was born April 9, 1978, in north London, where she still lives with her mother. Actually, she moved away from home for a while, and only returned last year, partly because she missed her mum, but also because it made life easier, since she was gone a lot. One item she did buy on moving back in was a full-size bed, so she could finally spread out and sleep in her favorite starfish position—not the easiest thing to do in a twin.

Unlike the others, Rachel didn't have a performing background before auditioning for the Club. That didn't mean she'd never loved it, though. In fact, beginning when she was five, Rachel had taken dance and drama classes every week for several years, and had major dreams of becoming a pop star—her favorite viewing was the British chart show *Top of the Pops*, when she imagined herself up there singing one of her hits—a dream that's become reality a few times now!

While she never pursued anything with dance, something else did attract her—modeling. She'd always enjoyed clothes and jewelry (in fact, she was often told off at school for wearing so much jewelry). People had told her how lovely she was, and that she should become a model, and after a while she began to seriously consider it. When she was fifteen, she saw a modeling contest and entered it. She was one of some five thousand girls to enter, however, so the odds weren't good. But she beat them all to win, and began to do some magazine and catalogue shoots. It was hardly the big time of Cindy Crawford or Naomi Campbell, but it was a start. And doing it all made Rachel realize she was very interested in fashion. She loved clothes (well, just like any other girl), but she was also interested in the business of fashion.

So she applied to fashion school, where she could really learn the ins and outs of the trade, and was accepted, beginning when she was sixteen. It was a two-year course, and at the end of it she managed to find a job doing public relations for a fashion company. While it wasn't quite as glamorous as modeling the clothes, it was steady work, and Rachel enjoyed being involved with the whole fashion world (and probably received a discount on all the trendy gear, too).

And it was through the fashion company that she met a couple of people from 19 Management, who suggested she audition for S Club 7. Well, that was about as close to her dream of being a pop star as she was likely to get, and there was nothing to lose by doing it, so Rachel did audition. She must have been one of the last people to do so; whereas the others had to wait months for an answer, she learned within two weeks that she had been accepted. The girl who'd wanted to be on *Top of the Pops* was going to be in a real band.

Rachel knew none of the others, but during their couple of weeks in Italy, she got to know them all very well, and proved herself to be a natural at the singing and acting, while the dance classes she'd taken when younger stood her in excellent stead for that part of the job. She wasn't shy, either, which was just as well, or she'd never have made herself heard over the noise of the others.

It is somewhat true that Rachel has a fashion obsession. But—and this is a big but—she can make fun of herself there too, and not take it all too seriously. Yes, she has a lot of clothes, but they're certainly not all with major designer labels. How on earth would she afford that? The show's producers couldn't afford to swing for that sort of stock. Actually, the clothes Rachel owns come from the high street stores, clothes based on the designer stuff, some of it very well done. For all that, though, the one item of clothing Rachel will never throw away, she insists, is "my jeans, because they're comfy and go with everything."

To be fair, you're not going to spot Rachel performing in a skirt and heels, and that would certainly be inappropriate for the show, where dressed-down is dressed up. But whatever she's wearing, she takes a real pride in her appearance. She knows what's classy and what's tacky (gloves with those little bobbles, for instance).

On the show, Rachel comes across as a real airhead. But nothing could really be further from the truth. She's actually got it all very much together. Certainly she's the only member of the Club to have a working car at home, which means that when they're working in London, she ends up ferrying the others around. Also, in the final episode of *S Club 7 in Miami* that really was her driving the convertible. It scared her at first, since she'd never driven anything that big (cars in England tend to be very small), but after a few minutes out by herself, she had the hang of it, and during the filming did everything without an accident (for which the producers were no doubt very grateful!).

While she loves the acting, the highlight of each episode for Rachel is been the Club get to perform. It might get very tiring, running through a song endlessly for all the different camera angles, but there's still an energy about it that gets to her. So it's no surprise that when the Club do shows, she really feels it. One of her greatest memories is from when they were at the premiere of their special, *Back to the Fifties*, at the Odeon in Leicester Square, London, where they'd also be performing live.

"We were in a hotel room looking out of the window so nobody could see us and we could see thousands of people queueing. That was a really amazing feeling. I felt a bit choked!"

That night, just to show they didn't take themselves especially seriously, once the screening had finished, there was another movie of outtakes from the special, which didn't always show the Club at their very best. How many bands these days would do *that*?

Rachel is very much a city person. Having grown up in London, she's used to the noise and bustle of a city, to the extent she becomes somewhat uncomfortable out in the country, especially if she's stuck in a village where the only clothes store might be a thrift shop whose garments are aimed at middle-aged women. But give her somewhere with a mall, and watch that frown turn into a smile. The first Sunday that the Club had off in Miami, where did she spend her time? In a mall, of course, and she loved every minute of it. Britain doesn't really have a mall culture the way America does. There are malls, but they're few and far between, and generally stuck outside the cities, pretty much away from things. And it's only in recent years that the idea of a mall has even arrived in England. So to have an entire day to look around, seeing names she'd never find in the UK (and probably prices lower than she'd hoped for, since clothes, especially American clothes, tend to be very expensive in England) made Rachel's heart beat a lot faster.

Something else makes her heart beat faster too—her boyfriend. She and Jo are the only ones of this crew to have steady dates, although it hasn't been easy with her being gone so much. However, it's worthwhile, and they've managed to keep it going through all the work, and through Rachel's rise to fame (a lot of girls dream about being on *Top of the Pops*, but few get to make their dreams a reality). About all you can say is that he's a very patient man (and a lucky one, too, since Rachel is really a sweetheart). In the show she might have been complaining because her boyfriend never wrote, but in real life there were letters flying back and forth across the Atlantic with great regularity. As if that wasn't quite enough, she spent loads of money calling him every day. Is that true love or what? So does this mean wedding bells in the near future? Probably not. With Rachel gone so much, it wouldn't be the best way to start married life, would it?

While Rachel, unlike Jo or Jon, doesn't sport any tattoos, she does have a piercing. Like Jo, she got her belly button pierced (hers is quite subtle—you have to look carefully to see the decoration). It's something that isn't as obvious as, say, a lip or an eyebrow, and more easily covered up. But it's almost impossible to think of Rachel actually piercing any part of her face—or any member of the Club, for that matter. It just doesn't seem like their kind of style.

Perhaps the biggest thrill for Rachel came when the Club went to New York to promote the show. If there was any one place she'd always wanted to visit, this was it. For her, it was like being taken to paradise, what with all the shopping possibilities around. Where could she begin? That question became especially important since the Club didn't have too much time there, and had a lot of commitments to fulfill on their schedule. Needless to say, though, the girl found the time to hit a few stores and buy a few things for herself.

And while they were in Los Angeles, Rachel went somewhere no other member of the Club had been—to a party at the Playboy Mansion, put on by the publisher of *Playboy*, Hugh Hefner.

"The daughter of my boyfriend's boss knew the people who organized it," she explained. "Girls were running around half naked on the stage for this old man. Not me, though!" It might have been swanky, but it definitely wasn't her kind of thing—and not exactly what she had in mind when the word party had been mentioned.

For all the airs and graces her character puts on, Rachel is actually quite down to earth, apart from the fact she loves clothes and makeup. On the show, she's the one who seems to attract the blokes like a magnet, but she doesn't even really look at other guys in real life; she's happy with her honey. And she's more than capable of looking beyond herself, joining with the others in the Club to support the World Wildlife Fund, with her big cause being the Siberian tiger (although she probably won't be petting one soon).

More than anything else, though, she loves her mum, which was the primary reason for moving back home. Being out on your own is great, but nothing beats a mother's touch and pampering when you've been traveling. Or having your dinner cooked and waiting when you get home after a hard day. Even if Rachel doesn't have quite as much freedom as she did before (and maybe not as much closet space, either), the compensations greatly outweigh the disadvantages. And it was pictures of her mother and her boyfriend that Rachel kept by her bedside in Miami to remind her of home.

Coming into the Club with no professional experience meant that Rachel had a pretty steep learning curve in the beginning. But all those dance and drama classes she'd taken made a huge difference, and these days you'd never know she hadn't been a professional entertainer all her life. Given that both the vocal lines and choreography on the songs are quite complex, it made for a lot to be taken in very quickly, especially considering the band went straight into the studio after their initial rehearsals to make their debut album.

Actually, it's hard to think of Rachel as anything but a star these days, almost as if she was born to the role—and it has to be admitted that it suits her perfectly. But, even though she loves it, the traveling and work do take their toll. A girl needs her beauty sleep, and that's been difficult to find for the last year, what with everything in the band's datebook. Give her a day off now, and rather than waking up early to go shopping, Rachel is a likely as the others to spend a lot of it in bed, just trying to catch up on her rest. Still, they have so much fun when they're together that's there's no doubt it's all worthwhile.

While she enjoyed all the filming, Rachel did have one favorite episode from the first season of *S Club 7 in Miami*. It was when the band "got to wear seventies outfits. I had a wicked minidress, knee-high boots, a wig, false eyelashes, and loads of glitter. It was excellent!"

While she's always seen on the show with hair that's straight and has lots of body, that's not quite her natural look. If you were to see Rachel first thing in the morning, there'd be some definite waves in her hair. She has them straightened out when she's in makeup, which is why she takes longer there than any of the others (at least, that's her excuse).

So far, being part of the Club has been a great trip for Rachel, and it's yet to continue for a long time. This is the most fun she's had in her life, so great that at times she can hardly believe she's getting paid to do it! She knows how lucky she is, and that lots of other girls would give anything to be in her shoes.

Smart and sensitive, unlike the Rachel on the show, Rachel has shown, too, that she has some excellent comic timing. She's a bit like Phoebe on *Friends* in a way, not always quite there—and playing that isn't always easy.

But Rachel has pulled it off very well indeed (as well as
creating a new stereotype, the dumb brunette). From obscurity to stardom, Rachel Stevens has steered a very
straight path indeed.

BRADLEY

WHAT CAN you say about Bradley McIntosh? The others give him a lot of grief, which on the show he generally deserves. He loves the ladies and he loves music, not necessarily (but probably) in that order. He's the real clown of the bunch, and also the one who loves his sleep far more than any of the others—in fact, in real life, he's actually perfected the idea of sleeping standing up; anywhere, anytime, Bradley can take a nap.

Like Rachel, he didn't have a professional performing background before joining the Club. He'd been in bands with some friends and family, one of which was called Crisp, and he had actually sung backup on a few radio jingles, but nothing that could be considered major. He'd rarely performed in front of an audience (his bands were more ideas than real entities), or made a record of his own. What he did have was a lot of enthusiasm and a great deal of talent.

Bradley, who's also known to the others as either Brad or Tosh, was born on August 8, 1981. From the very beginning, music was in his veins, since his parents were both musicians. His mum and dad played together in a reggae band that had a few hits. It was a big lineup, with seven instruments, and when they went on tour around the United Kingdom, little Bradley would go along with

them. It certainly prepared him early for the nomadic life
he's living now!

Music just came naturally to Bradley, and from a very
early age he loved it. In his room he'd practice being a
performer by singing along to old Jackson Five records.
In fact, when he was eight, he locked himself in his room
and wouldn't come out until he'd learned some Jackson
Five and Michael Jackson songs! After his parents' band
broke up (his mum has sung backup on some Ace of
Base records), his father opened a recording studio, and
Bradley would help him there, doing small jobs at first,
then bigger ones as he became more familiar with the
equipment. It never occured to him that he'd be anything
but a singer, although how that would happen didn't really seem to occupy his thoughts—he just believed it
would.

His dad's studio did all kinds of work, from recording
bands and singers to radio jingles, and that was where
Bradley got his taste of recording, doing some backup
vocals. That he had a good voice was undeniable. But
was it good enough? He certainly believed so, and decided, with the blessing of his parents, to pursue it as a
career, even though he might possibly have had a future
as a graphic designer. Leaving school at sixteen, he supported himself with a number of jobs, including working
in a few fast-food places, while going to various auditions.

Finally he heard about S Club 7, and sent in a demo
tape he'd done with his father, where he sang a version
of the Dru Hill song, "5 Steps." He had the voice, he had
the look, and he was in, and ready to go to Italy. It was
a sweet deal, and it has to be said that Bradley loves it—
when he can actually wake up enough to take part, of
course!

Of all the seven, Bradley is probably closest to the
person he portrays on television.

"What you see on-screen is very much the real me,"
he laughed. Which means late, messy, and a lot of other

things the rest of the crew like to make fun of him about. But it's all in good fun. They've very much taken him under their wing—he's a lovable cheeky chappie.

He's certainly pulled his weight, and shown himself to be a natural comedian, which came as something of a shock to him.

"I didn't know before watching myself back, because I hadn't realized my character was quite so funny."

But he is, and so is Bradley. Whether he's with the Club, or back home hanging with his posse of friends, whom he calls his "Bredrins," which is Jamaican patois for "brethren," he's a real cutup. Jo's taken it upon herself to make sure he keeps in line, but that's a pretty tall order. She only does it because he's a good mate, almost like a little brother to her, and she doesn't want him getting into too much trouble.

Since he's still young—and certainly very young at heart—Brad sometimes cracks the others up during filming, which doesn't leave the director best-pleased with him. But it's all due to a natural exuberance, and a love of life and everything in it. He's learning and getting there, and when he's serious, no one gives it more than Bradley does. For all his joking around, he's one hundred percent committed to the Club.

He definitely does have a problem with those early morning wake-up calls. Six-thirty in the morning seems disgustingly early to him (as it does to most people, really), so you can imagine what he was like when they had to get up at three A.M. or two-thirty. "I really *love* sleeping," he said with a passion. To him, midday is approaching a civilized time to wake up and consider the day. Still, with a lot of prodding and pushing, he's managed not to be too late so far. And once he's fully awake, it's like having a whirlwind of energy in the room. He's always talking, interrupting other people's conversations, wanting to say something, to add his voice into the mix.

When the Club have some free time on the road, and they're not out somewhere partying or shopping, you're most likely to find Bradley in front of the television with his PlayStation. He loves it, and he's willing to take on, and probably beat, all comers in the football (that's English football, not American) or racing games; he's become quite the expert. No one in the Club can beat him. But they love it when he plays, because it helps keep him quiet for a while! So it's one activity of Bradley's that's most definitely encouraged.

One thing the others definitely do not do is leave Bradley in charge of things, as in looking after their gear. Not unless they want it to vanish, that is. There's no one better in the Club at losing things than him. He doesn't do it deliberately, of course; it simply seems to happen. In Miami he managed to lose a bag that contained all the CDs he'd brought with him (and that was quite a few), which meant going out and replacing them all. Not that he exactly minded the shopping to find them again. Bradley is the boy who was born to shop.

He can spend hours going through the stores and trying on all the latest designer clothes—he's almost as bad as Rachel in that regard! Everyone has their own idea of fashion, and while Bradley tends toward the casual, there's one thing you'll *never* see him wearing, and that's a pair of sandals, just way too dressed down for him. But get him in those designer clothes and give him an evening, and he'll be out, clubbing it, and trying—and probably succeeding—in chatting up some girls.

You'd think, in Florida, with all the girls sunning themselves on the beach, Bradley would have broken more than a few hearts. But there wasn't anywhere near as much opportunity as he'd hoped. The series was being filmed in an area close to a retirement village, so there weren't too many girls for Bradley to try out his lines and his charm (and let's not forget that smile!) on. He had to wait until there was a night off, then head into South Beach to work his magic.

Wherever there were girls, Bradley managed to find them and ask them out, though. And they'd accept. He

was (and still is) often dating a few at a time, although
he swears he's going to try and just keep it down to one
(especially with Jo pulling hard at his leash, so he doesn't
cheat on anyone). But it's nothing serious with him, just
dating. He loves the ladies, that's what it is. You'll never
find him far from his cell phone (known in England as a
mobile phone), so the girls can call him (and note *they're*
calling him, not the other way 'round!). If you want to
make Bradley happy, just have him around "good music
and sexy ladies," and he's instantly smiling, ready to
dance and make a move—nothing shy about Bradley!
Needless to say, it'll be a remarkable girl who ties Bradley down, and he's certainly not looking for that yet.
With him gone so much, it would be totally unfair on the
other person. And given the way Bradley reacts whenever
he sees a pretty face, the temptation for him would be
excruciating—Jo would have to be watching him 24/7.

While he'll eat almost anything, give him a choice and
he'll go for Jamaican food (some tasty jerk chicken) or
stuff he learned to love in America—Mexican and Thai
cuisines. Not that he'd really cook them, but he definitely
knows how to order in. So if you pop around for dinner,
you'd better be prepared for something just a little on the
exotic side. And there's certainly nothing wrong with
that.

All his trips to the States have been a revelation to
Bradley. He thought nothing could beat Florida until he
hit the West Coast. San Francisco was excellent, totally
beautiful, but LA was it. It was wicked. Not only was
there lots of sun, and beaches close by, but it was a major
city with lots of stores and clubs, everything he could
wish for in a single place. And New York was brilliant,
too. Bradley absorbed a lot of American culture (well,
people in a lot of places have, thanks to global culture,
led by America), including some of the language. So
you'd find him going, " 'Hey, whassup? How're ya
doin'?' when I'm talking to the crew." Unlike the others,
though, who all wanted to sound very English, Bradley

took the phrases back home with him to use on his posse and his friends. What sounds everyday in one place can seem quite cool in another.

Back in England, Bradley still lives with his parents. It's easier than finding a place—and given how messy Bradley can be, the thought of the way his own place would look is enough to make anyone cringe. Like the others, though, he's never there for long; there are simply too many demands on his time these days. He's either jetting from one continent to another or in the recording studio, making a video, or hanging with his friends, going out places.

Even though it cuts heavily into his sleep time, Bradley certainly isn't complaining about the work he has to do as part of the Club. It was his dream to become a singer, and now he's doing it big-time—let's face it, it doesn't come any bigger than some top singles and an album that went all the way to number two!

So this is it for him. Surrounded by six close mates, he's part of a portable party. And it's everything he dreamed it would be. He's getting to see the world, he's recognized where he goes, and life is absolutely brilliant! Maybe even more than the others, he makes all the hard work seem easy, when, of course, it's not. There's a lot of waiting and boredom between shots, and the days of filming can be very long. So, like the others, he's perfected the art of the catnap. The only difference is that he's taken it one step further. While the others have to be lying down, or at least sitting, to fall asleep, Bradley can just lean against a wall and drop off. Try it sometime—it's a great skill to be able to be able to do it and not fall down!

If such a thing as a cool meter existed, Bradley would score a hundred. Even when he's goofing around, there's just an air of coolness about him. And you add to that the fact that he can also play the drums with his teeth (don't ask!), and you've got a pretty remarkable individual.

Probably none of the show's characters are closer to reality than Bradley's. And that's not because he can't act, although he tends to come across as more of a natural performer than anything forced. But when that natural personality is so strong, why try to hide it? Granted, all of the members of the Club have strong personalities, but Bradley's somehow manages to shine through even when he's not even saying anything. That's a rare gift, and really marks him out as someone with big star potential.

Of course, he already *is* a star, and he has no plans or desires to leave the fold. Since his ambition was always to sing, he's doing that, and loads more besides, which makes him a very happy bunny indeed. He's had the chance to develop talents he never even knew he had, and there's no doubt he loves what he does.

Everyone hoped the Club would be big, but in reality there was no way of knowing for sure that it would happen. So when their singles all went mega in Britain, and the album took off, everyone was thrilled, most especially Bradley, since he was essentially following in the family business by making records.

His parents are very proud of him (as is his little sister). But all the success hasn't gone to his head. He's still just a regular bloke who does regular things in the few moments he's not working. Give him Sunday lunch at his mum's and he's happy. However, get him glancing in the mirror at his eyebrows, and he's not so smiley—for some weird reason he dislikes his eyebrows! Like the others in the Club, he's firmly committed to the world Wildlife Fund cause, and he picked the hyacinth macaw to help.

For all the scrapes he gets in now and again on the show because of his exuberance and sense of humor, the others stop him from going over the top, just as they do in real life. Bradley's a good soul, just so full of life that it bubbles out of him and overflows. Except when he's sleeping, he seems to be "on" all the time, and that's just his way. He can chill; it simply doesn't happen that often.

And that's Bradley. A great voice, lots of charm (as many ladies have found out!), and the kind of humor that would have you laughing far too hard all the time. The odds are that, if he wants it, he'll still be a star twenty years from now, and that's a pretty big claim to make of anyone. But Bradley can live up to it.

TINA

TINA BARRETT might be nicknamed Tina Bell or Teeny,
but don't go thinking that means she's small; in fact she's
the tallest girl in the Club, up there with the boys in
height. But tall doesn't equate to clumsy, either. Of all
of them, Tina moves with the most grace, in a part because she trained for years as a dancer, which was how
she was making her living before she auditioned for the
Club.

Tina's also the oldest member of the Club, born on
September 16, 1976. She's far from running out of energy, though. She can be as hyper as any of them, and
sometimes (although she insists age has nothing to do
with it) the bossiest of the lot.

From a very young age, Tina was fascinated with
dancing. She began taking ballet classes almost as soon
as she could walk, and showed quite a precocious talent
for all forms of dancing—she was a complete natural. So
having her go to the London Arts Education School
seemed a perfect move, since it was geared to kids who
had special talents in different artistic fields, giving them
a real chance to develop them while still offering a good,
all-around education.

Certainly it gave Tina opportunities to move forward
as a dancer that she'd only have had in specialized af-

terschool classes otherwise, and being around others like herself helped boost her confidence, realizing she wasn't alone or some sort of freak.

Her height and her looks didn't hurt her, either, and it was because of them that she got a couple of jobs as a model, doing a fashion show for Wella, and then on television (her first TV spot!), showing clothes on *Clothes Show Live*. And then came her second television gig, working as a dancer on a Disney special.

Actually, television would play quite a role in her career. Through her agent, Tina got some work in ads, including one for a brand of chewing gum, which involved the rather uncomfortable task of being outside in a swimsuit in the middle of winter for the shoot—not exactly something you'd do for fun. And in another ad, she played a roof, of all things (still, you could say she was starting at the top . . .). It was all work, and that was good. She appeared as a dancer on *Top of the Pops* (which made her the first member of the Club to be on the show, really), and was in a video by top pop band Pulp, as well as appearing on the British morning television show, *This Morning*. All in all, she had a pretty good resume behind her, although it wasn't the kind of thing that was making her rich, by any means. And then "one of my agents set me up for the S Club 7 thing and I went on auditions and eventually got in."

Like most of the others, it took a long time between audition and acceptance. But that was simply because so many people tried out, and the management wanted to be certain they were making the right choices. Once Tina was in, however, she was totally behind the idea, and a fully committed member of the band.

Since she loves clothes, she immediately hit if off with Rachel. But Tina has something she loves even more than clothes, and that's shoes. She has over thirty pairs, and it's a collection she's adding to constantly. And who can blame her? After all, a girl simply can't have too many shoes. You see something that goes perfectly with a par-

ticular outfit, or will be right for a special occasion—you
know how it is.

Although Tina comes across on the show as the re-
served one, in real life she's not quite that way. In her
own, slightly quiet way, she has a great laugh, with a
sense of humor that's unique—so unique that a lot of
people don't always get it. But that's fine. Once you get
used to it, she can be very funny indeed. And there's also
another, more physical side to her humor: "I do things
like pinch my friends' bums, just for a laugh."

Back in London, Tina shares an apartment with a
friend in Hammersmith, which isn't quite the trendiest
part of the capital, but one that suits her just fine. In fact,
she loves it there, and it's certainly handy enough for
everything she wants, including going to shows and clubbing. Given her choice, she'll listen to bands like Prodigy
and Busta Rhymes, as well as the Fugees. (Wyclef Jean
of the Fugees was hanging in Miami while the Club were
busy filming, but there was no free time for Tina to go
Fugee-spotting, which saddened her. But she made up for
it later with a trip to go shopping there. In the end, however, she returned with very little new stuff, determined
to be a good girl and not spend *all* her money.) And
while she's been known to dis Hanson on the show, in
real life she doesn't mind them that much—although she
doesn't own any of their CDs.

One of the great joys of filming the series was the
chance to dress up. Tina absolutely loved getting into
seventies gear, or dressing up like a space alien, a cow-
girl, and in a Spanish outfit. In a lot of ways it was like
being a kid again and playing make-believe, only getting
paid for it, which can never be bad. It certainly made the
long hours each day a lot more fun for her, and added a
great deal of variety.

When you watch the musical numbers in the show,
watch Tina carefully, and you'll notice the natural grace
with which she moves. That all comes from her years of
training as a dancer, which is still how she primarily sees

herself, even though she really has a multifaceted career these days, as an actress and singer, too.

While she might seem a little over the top at times on the show, to the point of being quite strident when she gets her temper up, in real life Tina is pretty much of a pussycat, the one who's least like her character on the show (she doesn't have many accidents in real life, either). She's actually a bit of a homebody in her free time, and that's not just because she's always tired from Club work. She likes to be back in Hammersmith, in her flat, putting her feet up and relaxing.

She missed her parents while she was in Florida filming, but since she's been living away from home for a while, for her it wasn't as acute as it was for a couple of the younger members. When she got home she called her folks, and when she'd rested up, she went over to see them.

Much as she likes her apartment, though, she also loves to be on the move. "I like traveling and being away from home," she said. She was the only one not to bring anything from home to Florida. She wanted the experience to be total, not to have her heartstrings dragged back to London every time she picked up a photograph. Of course, that didn't mean she never missed anything about England. But she was able to take the new experience for what it was—a challenge and a complete immersion in a new culture.

One thing she'd have loved to have done was get a good Florida tan, and to be able to go back home all bronze and shiny. Lovely as the idea was, it simply wasn't practical. For a start, there wasn't the free time to lounge around and sunbathe. And secondly, it wouldn't have looked very good to have had them pale in one scene and all dark in the next—the shows weren't all shot one after another, and scenes from different shows would sometimes be filmed on the same day. So it was only when they were filming on the beach that they really got any sun, and even then they were all heavily leathered with sunscreen—those fair English skins weren't used to the hot Florida sun!

Being out in California, especially Los Angeles, was wonderful for Tina. Not just because she got to see Hollywood, and to film there, but because it meant she might be able to get a glimpse of two of her favorite stars. Tina just adores Johnny Depp and British actor Gary Oldman (who's done quite a bit of work in America). Well, maybe the star-spotting wasn't successful, but there was plenty she did get to see, and she loved it, just as she loved New York, with all its energy. And we probably shouldn't mention the range of shopping in either of those cities. Tina might have been good in Miami, but who could resist LA or NY?

One thing Tina doesn't have is a boyfriend. There's been no one special, and given how crazy her life is right now, it seems unlikely there'll be anyone on the immediate horizon. How do you sustain a relationship when you're constantly traveling and away from home for months at a time? It's a problem that not only members of the Club have, but anyone in a band that's successful. The simple answer is that you make some sacrifices, and that's what Tina's had to do, as well as all the others. Your career has to come first, if you're going to take it seriously. It's hard enough when you're starting out, with all the time and energy that requires, but it just gets worse as you become more famous—it's hard to find time for yourself, let alone for anyone else.

Like the others in the Club, to Tina sleep has become a valuable and rare commodity. Prior to this, she definitely wasn't used to being up at the crack of dawn or before. Now, she's learned to be ready pretty much anytime, anywhere, and to grab those power naps at every opportunity, because you don't know when the chance will come again.

It's a strange, and in many ways, an unnatural lifestyle, but Tina's adapted to it. While she might never have seen herself as a singer, at least when she was grow-

THE MEMBERS OF S CLUB 7 PARTICIPATE IN THE "WALK FOR WILDLIFE" AT THE WHIPSNADE ZOO IN THE UK.
(© SIMON MEAKER/ALL ACTION/RETNA)

S Club 7 proudly displays the WWF logo at the Whipsnade Zoo.
(© Theodore Wood/Camerapress/Retna)

HANNAH BELTS OUT A TUNE AT
THE T.V. HITS AWARD SHOW.
(© THEODORE WOOD/CAMERAPRESS/RETNA)

JO DISPLAYS SOME FANCY
DANCE MOVES ONSTAGE.
(© THEODORE WOOD/CAMERAPRESS/RETNA)

TINA GIVES AN ENERGETIC PER-
FORMANCE.
(© THEODORE WOOD/CAMERAPRESS/RETNA)

S CLUB 7 HAPPILY POSES WITH
AN ELEPHANT AT THE WHIPSNADE
ZOO.
(© THEODORE WOOD/CAMERAPRESS/RETNA)

THE MEMBERS OF THE GROUP ENJOY HANG-
ING OUT TOGETHER.
(© SIMON MEAKER/ALL ACTION/RETNA)

THEY LOOK SHARP ONSTAGE IN THEIR HIP OUTFITS AND BRIGHT SMILES.

(© NICKY J. SIMS/REDFERNS/RETNA)

ing up, she always had the desire to be up there, using her talent to entertain people—and that's exactly what she's doing. It's a calling, and one that demands a lot. You live on the faith that you're going to make it some-day, and until that point you take any job that might help. Most of them are just one-off bits of work that hopefully lead to more and more. But it's a risky game. Possibly dancers have it worse than anyone else. Since dance is so physically demanding, past the age of thirty their bod-ies are no longer as elastic as they were, which leaves a much smaller window of time in which to get known.

So for Tina, this is perfect. She gets the chance to dance—quite a lot, really—and do other things, too, to show the full range of her talents. And, as the real dancer, she can help the others with their moves, just as Jo can help her with her singing, and Hannah, Jon, and Paul can help her with her acting. They all work together to form a single unit—that's what the Club are about, and why they're inclusive rather than exclusive.

While Tina's always been dedicated to dancing, it wasn't the only thing she loved. In school she was an excellent artist, and could possibly have gone on to art school if she'd had the desire. But other things came first in her life, and we're all very glad now that they did.

If you're thinking Tina might be the same kind of party animal as Hannah (or even Jon), you might want to think again. If she was having a party, she'd be serving "cheese and pineapple on sticks, Kettle crisps [chips] and a bottle of ginger ale." Not exactly the wild life, but then Tina isn't the sort to waltz through life with total aban-don. She's worked very hard to get where she is now, and as a professional, she takes it all very seriously. Go-ing back, she'd never have dreamed she'd be singing on *Top of the Pops*, let alone have some number one hits. But life takes strange turns for everyone. In Tina's case, they've been very good and happy turns. After all, it's a long way from playing a roof to being a singing-dancing-acting machine in Florida!

So she certainly has no regrets about joining the Club, and like the others, no plans to leave, even though she is the oldest. The band's website might say NO ONE OVER 23 ADMITTED but there are plenty of exceptions to that rule, and the first is Tina herself.

She shares the social concerns of the rest of the band, and has put herself very firmly behind their World Wildlife Fund campaign, choosing as her animal the panda, probably the cuddliest of the lot (although you might not want to get too close; they're bigger than you imagine).

So while on the show, things seem to happen to Tina, in real life she's always been the one to make them happen. She's in control, without being overly-controlling. She's happy, as friendly as a puppy, and every bit as charming as a princess. This has been something of a wild ride for her, and she loves the fact that from day to day she doesn't know what might be coming next. It's an adventure, and she's enjoying it for all it's worth.

AND THAT'S the band, the Club. While they're all so different, they do share some common traits. They're all dedicated to what they do. They're ambitious—they wouldn't even have gone to the auditions if they weren't. And, it goes without saying, they're all talented. They have the fame, but they've worked hard for it, and they're still working incredibly hard—harder than ever, really. That means a lot of sacrifices, from having any kind of personal life, right down to a good night's sleep. But when something turns out to be so right, and so much fun, it's worth everything, really.

PART TWO

S CLUB 7

EVERYWHERE

CHAPTER ONE

HOW DO you put a band together? Usually it's a group of individuals who come together of their own accord, through friendship, because they want to make the same kind of music. They have a single goal, and a lot in common. They practice, work hard, and try to become successful doing something they love.

But that's not the only way. In the history of pop music, groups have been manufactured, its members put together by someone else with the idea of commercial success. The people chosen were there for their talents or their personalities. Perhaps the best example before the 1990s was the Monkees, who, in the sixties, not only had international pop smashes, but also a wildly successful television series.

But it was in the nineties that manufactured bands really took off. The Spice Girls, perhaps the biggest manufactured band of all time, were mega. But they were put together by girls answering an ad in a British trade paper. Some of the top boy bands came together in similar ways, too. So is it wrong to do things that way, to tinker with the elements and try to find the right mix rather than letting a band develop organically?

Of course not. The bottom line is that it all depends on the chemistry of the members. If something isn't working, it's quite apparent to everyone—not the least to those who might buy the records.

S Club 7 are a manufactured band. It's something no one has tried to hide or deny. And why should they? It's the truth, and they're honest people. They were put together by Simon Fuller, who'd seen his initial creation, the Spice Girls, go on to bigger and better things with other people. But he understood how it was done, and decided to try again—but adding a twist. Not only would he put together a band that could sing and put out records, he'd have them on television too, in their own series.

Yes, it was definitely shades of the Monkees. But that was something no one had tried to recapture. And although *The Monkees* borrowed its zaniness and fast-cut technique from the first two Beatles' movies, it became a success on its own terms. That, however, had been more than thirty years ago. There was a huge entertainment void in the market that a similar show could fill, and who better to do it than a pop band that could also act?

Fuller's company, 19 Management, was big. Apart from a number of pop stars, they also handled sports personalities, celebrities, and number of instantly recognizable people. That meant they had clout and influence in the business. People listened when they had ideas. And people were willing to listen to this idea.

Like anything else, it was a gamble. But you have to take risks to move ahead. This, however, was something huge. It wasn't just a case of putting a band together and seeing what happened. All the pieces had to be in place. There'd be songs ready and waiting to be recorded. Scripts for the show would have to be written, and all the fine details of filming would have to be sorted out. In other words, this was going to be a major deal.

And that meant there was no room for error. In the end it all came down to the people who might buy the records and watch the show, but everything up to that point had to be as perfect as it could be. The biggest part of that was finding exactly the right combination of people to be in the band.

The only way to do that was to see as many different people as possible—singers, actors, dancers, looking for people who had the right natural spark. That meant putting ads in the trade papers, as well as scouring all over for people who might fit the bill. This was, after all, a huge project.

It would take a long time to come up with the seven people who'd comprise the Club. There were endless auditions, a ton of demo tapes to be listened to. Months and months of work went into the process. For some people who tried out, it was, quite literally, months before they heard they were in. But that was what it took to get it right. Not only did it have to be a group of people who seemed like they'd get along well together, but their talents had to complement each other—no small feat.

But finally they'd come up with everyone. And, let's face it, seven was a pretty big number to come up with, making them the biggest band around in terms of sheer numbers. They met each other for the first time at London's Heathrow airport, preparing to fly out to Italy, where they'd have the time to get to know each other, and to rehearse for their very first project—making an album.

Paul and Hannah had known each other for a few years, but for the others, this was all brand new. They had their different talents and abilities, but could they work together? Would it gel? By the time the plane touched down in Italy, the answer seemed like a resounding yes. They were all bubbly, overjoyed to have been chosen, full of energy, and ready to work.

So why take them to Italy, far from home, to rehearse? Well, it was the far from home bit that was the key. In another country, where none of them spoke the language, there would be no distractions, no family or friends liable

to drop around. They could be isolated, get to know each
other properly, and spend two weeks really focusing on
the work at hand. In many ways, it was a rehearsal for
the amount of work they'd have to put in down the line,
once the filming of the show began. And it gave the
bosses a chance to make sure everyone did work well
together, before it was too late.

There turned out to be no worries on that score. They
bonded like a family, teasing each other, but still looking
out for each other. It quickly seemed as if they'd known
each other all their lives, and they threw themselves into
learning the songs and the harmonies they needed—not
to mention a fair bit of choreography. Anyone who'd
been thinking the two weeks in Italy was going to be a
great vacation was wrong, wrong, wrong. Instead it was
work, work, work, from morning until long after dark.

There were plenty of songs to be learned, and the harmonies were often complex, requiring a great deal of
work on everyone's part, going over them again and
again until they were perfect.

And then there was the dancing. Only Tina and Rachel
had dance experience, so for the rest of the crew it meant
a very steep learning curve. But they were up for it, and
by the time they were ready to come home, everything
was down.

From there, they were whisked into the studio. Only
Jo had gone through this experience before, and she was
hoping this would be as successful—no, *more* successful—than that, when she'd made a single that hit the
charts in Germany. Bradley's studio experience had been
limited to backup vocals—not quite the same thing.

Studio recording demands perfection. Nothing less
works, because the mistakes become quite apparent when
you listen to a CD, or to a track on playback. And that
was where all the effort in Italy paid off. Everything was
still very fresh in their minds. They all knew exactly what
they had to do, and did it. That's not to say it was always
easy. With so many voices to record, and quite a number

of tracks to do, they ended up spending several weeks in the studio, making what would be their first album and their singles. They hadn't had a hand in writing the material, but throughout music history, performers have more often recorded the work of other writers than their own songs. There'd be time for that—if any of them even showed an inclination for writing—later on. The main thing was to get this exactly right.

Meanwhile, behind the scenes, the people who'd put together the Club were working out all the details of filming the show in Florida—as well as selling the idea to television networks around in the world. In Britain, the BBC had agreed to air it. In America, Fox Family was very interested.

"When I heard about the creative team that was putting this together, we got really excited about its potential," said Fox Family senior vice president Joel Andryc. "We're looking for S Club 7 to be as big, if not bigger, than some of the recent groups that came out of the UK."

That was putting a heavy weight on the shoulders of seven young people who'd yet to start filming the series or even release their first record. And, in the end, it did all depend on them. The creative team and the marketing people could do everything possible, but if the faces and voices didn't appeal to people who'd watch the show and buy the records, then it didn't really matter. That was the very bottom line of it all.

You do everything possible to ensure success. But in the end you have to have that faith that it will work. To help things along, some top writing talent was brought in for the show. Some of the people who were penning scripts had worked on some very highly-rated series like *Fresh Prince of Bel Air, Friends*, as well as the British comedy *Red Dwarf* and also the Spice Girls' movie, *Spiceworld*. No one was trying to cut corners.

But while all that was being set up, filming was still quite a way away. Rachel, Bradley, Hannah, Paul, Jo,

Jon, and Tina were getting a little time off, which by now they desperately needed.

The thing to understand is that all this was worked out like a military operation. The Club might have been the visible aspect of it all, and the ones everyone would relate to and see, but like the iceberg in *Titanic*, most of what was going on wasn't really open for viewing.

It was now early in 1999.

While the Club got to chill, preparations were going on in Florida, and auditions were being held for the American roles—specifically Howard (played by Alfie Wise, a veteran actor whose credits include *Cannonball Run*). Everything, including filming crews, all the locations, every single item, needed to be in place by the time the Club arrived to begin work on the series in February.

There was already a small buzz going around in the British press about the Club—advance publicity was never a bad thing. But so far a buzz was all it could be. No record would be released until later in the year, although the series would begin airing in England in the spring. After that, it was hoped, S Club 7 would be a big enough name to give a hit single or two. But "hoped" was the apt word. There was no way to guarantee that. They could put out the record, but they couldn't force anyone to buy it. Only time would tell if it was all going to turn out fine, or if this was going to be a gigantic waste of time and money.

For all the members of the Club, the downtime gave them a chance to see their families and friends before heading off to the States. They knew it was going to be a long, hectic trip, although spending February and March in the Florida sun didn't sound too much like hardship to the people they told. After the gray skies and rain of England, anything would seem like a relief, especially when it included a lot of sand and surf. But they knew how hard they'd be working, and that it would be nothing like a vacation. They already had a good idea from the kind of schedule they'd been on. They wanted to make it big, and they knew that involved a great deal of work. For the last few months it was as if they'd been living in a pressure cooker. Everything had to be right, and they were the ones on the spot, who had to get it all just so!

Filming a television series is stressful enough at the best of times. To do a whole season of shows, thirteen of them, in a couple of months, is a good way to raise the stress level as high as possible.

The premise behind the show was pretty simple. The band's somewhat sleazy manager, Danny Parsons, wasn't doing them much good. They wanted to work, and he wasn't getting them any gigs. To appease them a little, he promised to find them work in America—building it up more than it really was, of course. So the band flew off to Florida, expecting to be working at a top hotel, only to find Howard and the Florida Paradise. Where they'd expected only to entertain, they found themselves doing everything, from cleaning to waiting tables, and singing in the evenings. The series chronicled their adventures while working at the hotel, the ups and downs they had with Howard, some side trips—and, of course, plenty of music, with at least one song in each show.

It wasn't high art or high drama. It was a fun show, aimed at kids. Often goofy, always comic, it played up the differences between Britain and America in grand style, made it seem like the Club were having fun no matter what they ended up doing, and gave them a chance to showcase their singing and dancing, as well as their acting.

It was *The Monkees* for the millennium. That show had portrayed a band trying to find work, having all kinds of mad, deliberately zany adventures—and it gave them the chance to play at least one song per episode. As a show it had been hugely popular, helping to turn the Monkees into a band of international proportions, with hits all over the globe. There was even a revival of interest in the nineties, when all the episodes appeared on video, and all the albums were remastered on CD. In all honesty, if S Club 7 could hit as well as the Monkees had done, they'd be laughing.

For Paul, Jon, and Hannah, acting was the easy part. It was what they did. But for the others, it was going to be nerve-wracking. Jo, in particular, felt like she took some time to fall into a groove, and that it wasn't until the fourth or fifth episode she began to feel comfortable with the idea of playing a character like herself on camera. After that she opened up a lot. Of course, that was one reason for making the characters so like the real people—or at least, into caricatures of the real people, emphasizing certain aspects of their personalities to make them funnier.

Even for the seasoned actors it was going to be incredibly hard work. Everyone knew that in advance. During their entire time in Florida they'd only get two full days off—that tells you just how hard they were working. For Rachel, Bradley, Jo, and Tina, whose experience of acting was minimal, it was going to require an awful lot of dedication.

CHAPTER TWO

MIAMI, FLORIDA. People have an image of the place. For some it's where people go to retire. For others, Florida means spring break. There's DisneyWorld. A few remember the eighties show, *Miami Vice*, which seemed to change the whole tone of cop shows on television. There's the South Beach area of the city, where all the beautiful people hang out, with its clubs, hotels, and expensive shops—all very trendy. There's the big Cuban section of town, famous now throughout the world.

And then there's Lauderdale by the Sea. Not so many people have heard of that. It's not actually in Miami, or even right next door. But it's a lot quieter, and that was what the producers needed. The way the show was shot, no one would know it wasn't really Miami.

There's no Florida Paradise Hotel, either. At least, there's no hotel of that name. But there is Villas by the Sea in Lauderdale by the Sea, and for a couple of months it became the Florida Paradise. But, through the trick of television, what viewers saw wasn't the whole hotel. Just parts of it were filmed. In fact, it's a huge complex of buildings covering quite a bit of ground—and each of the buildings has its own pool.

And, unlike the Florida Paradise, it's not run-down, either; it's perfectly lovely. The parts used for filming were deliberately made to look a bit on the desperate side to give the impression of a place just getting by.

Lauderdale by the Sea is a place that's popular with retirees who want to vacation in Florida. They like the fact that it's quiet, and that it's removed from all the hustle and bustle of Miami. There's ample sea and sand. And Villas by the Sea is a popular place for them to stay on vacation. In fact, there were quite a lot of other guests really using it as a hotel while filming was going on, and some of them even ended up having walk-on parts in the show!

For the Club, arriving there was like heaven. Jon might have missed the English rain, but he's also a sun worshipper, so he was also quite happy with that. And if they were going to be working their butts off, what better place to do it?

Of course the initial scenes were filmed in England, as the band confronted Danny Parsons (who was played by Gary Whelan—like Jon, a veteran of *EastEnders*), and then went to the airport to catch their flight. But the vast majority of the show would be made in the USA.

There wasn't even time for the guys to get over their jet lag before it was time to work. Their very first evening was spent going over the scripts for the next day's shooting. No rest for the wicked—although there certainly wasn't the time to be properly wicked.

Everyone was nervous the first day on the set, although Hannah, John, and Paul felt more confidence than the others. But it was still a case of getting used to their costars, and the way of working that the director had, as well as the sheer pace of everything. Since there was so much to do within such a short time frame, there wasn't the luxury of endless retakes. They had to be on their marks and word-perfect first time, if at all possible. So, if they seem a bit subdued in the first few episodes of the series, you can understand why—they were making the transition, not only to a new environment, but also to the idea of working for the camera.

But it worked out fine. Everyone was there to help them along, to make it all proceed smoothly. After all, it was in everyone's interest to make the show a success. Quite a few scenes were shot away from the hotel, and for that, local police acted as security—which meant that the Club soon became friends with the law (and definitely stayed on the right side of it).

However, you might be surprised to know that all the scenes shot in the boys' and girls' hotel rooms, where they lived in bunk beds, weren't shot in Florida at all. The interiors, as they're known, were actually filmed in London, before the Club flew out to Florida, then spliced in at the editing stage. All you can say is that it was a good job of duplicating the Florida sunshine in a London soundstage!

The real filming was a job that lasted from morning until night. Starting with makeup at the crack of dawn, the members of the Club had to be available until the end of the day, each and every single day. Often not all of them were needed, but they still had to be there, just in case. It was mad. And when filming finished for the day, there was still no chance to relax. Over dinner, and into the night, Rachel, Tina, Jon, Bradley, Hannah, Jon, and Jo were working on the scripts for the next day, going through the scenes and learning their lines. It was always late when they got to bed (and they actually all had rooms to themselves, not the dormitories of the show!), for just a few hours of sleep.

While they had the scripts to work from, at times members of the cast would suggest changes in the lines, and often the director was happy to include them. It made sense, really; who knew better than they how to speak and react to things? But, it has to be said, the writers did an excellent job of summing them up, creating the slightly fictionalized versions of their characters and getting much of their speech down perfectly.

It quickly became apparent that every day was going to be an adventure. The Club got to do things most people dream about, and probably the highlight for everyone was when they had the opportunity to swim with dolphins for the episode *How Deep Is Your Love?* It was the kind of experience to stay with them forever. For Jon and Hannah, especially, it was something of a dream come true—it was a thing they'd both wanted to do, and it left them completely speechless after having communed with the dolphins.

There were so many great times. It would have been easy for the veteran American actors who were part of the series to have looked down on them as a bunch of Brit kids, but everyone was as nice as could be. Alfie Wise, who played Howard, even made the gesture of getting each member of the Club a director's chair with his or her name stenciled on it. It was something he didn't need to do, and everyone appreciated the friendship.

But there was plenty of friendship in the air. No holiday romances—no time or energy for that—but Jon, Tina, Paul, Hannah, Jo, Bradley, and Rachel became good friends with the crew, the other actors, with so many people they were around every day. The series might have starred them, but that didn't mean they were stars. They didn't think of themselves that way, and there were absolutely no ego trips.

With police providing security, they got to know the boys in blue—but also the local firemen, too. At times the lights would trigger fire alarms, which would bring the fire crew racing. It didn't happen often—and probably just as well for everyone's sake—but it did give everyone a chance to get to know the local fire service.

While it was pretty much all work and no play, the guys did get a little time off for good behavior—or maybe bad behavior, depending on how you looked at it. Paul turned twenty-two while they were filming, so they took that night off for a real S Club party. And party they did—enough that they were dragging the following day. But what else are birthdays for, anyway? They headed into Miami and took on South Beach. They're still trying to figure out who won!

Of the two full days they had off, one was spent in Miami—well, they had to see it properly, didn't they? But for the other they didn't sleep or spend the time sunning themselves on the beach, just relaxing. They were up and at 'em early (it had become a habit by now) and rented a boat for the day to be able to look at Florida from the water. Bradley was the captain for the day— and they still made it back in one piece!—and it turned out to be exactly the kind of break they needed.

None of them had ever been under that kind of pressure before. Even when Jon was in *EastEnders*, he wasn't in every episode. Here they had to make almost two shows each week, with a lot of exterior filming, a lot of singing and dancing, and make sure it all came in under budget.

They also learned a lot of new skills. Prior to going to Florida, none of them had played volleyball before— which wasn't good news considering one episode had them in a volleyball match. But they ended up getting lessons from the pros before they played, then looking as if they really knew what they were doing.

None of it was easy, but they kept their spirits up and kept each other going. A lot of goofing around kept everything light, and the other people on the series were an absolute joy to work with, including fellow Brit Cathy Dennis. She'd had a career as a top pop star, with hits like "All Around The World," but now she was playing Jill Ward, an actress in a show called *Alien Hunter*, and a very New Age-y person. No singing for her this time around, but she did end up appearing in two episodes, including the pivotal final one.

It was hard to believe when they finally wrapped production on a Friday in late March. After working so hard for what seemed like so long, it was over, and they had an entire weekend in which to relax—and sleep. But while it was a relief to have everything complete, there was still a lot of sadness. They'd become close to every-one on the series, and a wrap (along with the wrap party) meant it was time to say goodbye to them all.

But even though the *series* was in the can, S Club 7 still had one more thing to do in Florida. After a weekend off, they had to film the video for "Bring It All Back" on Monday, and that meant an entire day in the sun, singing along with the music and performing the chore-ography time after time after time after time. In fact, it made the series look like a piece of cake.

It didn't help that it was a particularly hot day. After each take they had to change clothes, they were sweating so much (Bradley went through nine identical tee shirts over the course of the day), and Jon proved to be the first casualty, having to go into the trailer to rest, after dislocating his leg trying to do his famous flip. Now that was a major problem, since they only had one day to shoot. But he was a real trouper. After resting for twenty minutes, with ice on his leg, he came out and tried again—and this time nailed it on the first attempt, before completing the rest of the routine. Eventually, though, they finished it all. And there were some little technical tricks to help them. Where the dancing seems speeded up, the tape of the song was actually being played at half speed for them to move to—on playback it made it seem as if they were moving very fast.

With all that over, finally, they could pack their bags and head back to England, trading in the sunshine for gray skies and rain. Ah, to be home again . . .

They did, however, leave a bit of themselves in Flor-ida. You might remember the bar on the beach. It was actually built just for the show, but the people asked them to leave it up rather than tear it down. Given that the locals had been so wonderful, how could they have re-fused?

CHAPTER THREE

To BE home was to sleep. And sleep. And maybe have some sleep, too, as well as seeing their families after a long time away. For Jon it was a chance to see all the episodes of *Coronation Street* he'd missed while he was gone. There was so much they had to tell everybody about the things they'd seen and done.

In some ways, however, they didn't actually have to tell anyone, since no sooner were they back in Britain than the first episode of *S Club 7 in Miami* was aired by the BBC. It was very weird for all of them to sit and watch something they'd worked on so recently now in its finished state, and looking remarkably cool. A number of titles had been tossed around for the show, including *7 In Miami* (sort of a play on the old Enid Blyton children's books, once so popular in England) and *7 Up* (which didn't go too far, for obvious reasons). Everyone who'd worked on the show referred to it as *Miami 7*.

So now they were on the telly, and from the very first episode it was the top-rated children's show in the UK—a fact that surprised Jon, since he had no idea they even had charts for children's television. It aired in the late afternoon, after everyone was home from school and before the news, which has always been "children's hour" on British television.

The great thing was, although it was extremely popular with kids, teens and adults could enjoy it, too. It was most definitely PG, with nothing to offend, but plenty to amuse and entertain people of all ages. That made it something different. For parents, it brought back the days of watching *The Monkees*, and for teens who happened to be sitting there when their younger brothers and sisters turned on the TV, well, between the hunks, babes, sand, and surf, there was also some very appealing music.

From the show, everyone knew who Jon, Tina, Paul, Rachel, Bradley, Jo, and Hannah were—but they'd yet to make a real public appearance in their own country. That would change very quickly, as they began their first promotional tour for the show. It was two weeks of going from one end of Britain to the other in a minibus, talking to people in local radio, television, and press.

It was actually the most stressful time they'd had together. The drives were long, the minibus was cramped, and they were tired. But they made it through intact, thanks to their sense of humor. This was all part of the job, and they did it because it was a part of it all. And it wasn't *too* bad—there were still plenty of laughs along the way.

It allowed people to see who they really were, and to let everyone know the show was on—not that most people needed to be alerted. The word was already out in schools and among kids, and the viewing figures for the episodes kept growing and growing.

Then there was one incident that made everything about the trip worthwhile. They had a television in the minibus, which helped pass the time, although reception wasn't always the best. One show they always made sure to watch was *Top of the Pops*. After all, not only were they a band, but they all loved music. Tina had danced on the show before, and Paul had been in the audience once. So, on the week "Bring It All Back" was released, they were watching and completely stunned when their video was aired as an "exclusive." It was a cue for much screaming and shouting. The picture quality was awful, but that didn't matter—they were on *Top of the Pops*. It was yet another dream come true!

With the single out, it was time for more touring. They'd already had their first taste of fandom in Scotland, when kids besieged them at their hotel for autographs—which was pretty mind-boggling to them all—but that was just the beginning. They began playing roadshows all over the country, performing the song for the people who'd come out. Between that, and the popularity of the show, it was definitely having an effect on sales of the single, which was shooting up the chart.

It was an exhilarating feeling, playing to live audiences, and they all loved the buzz and the energy of it, even if it got crazy sometimes. There was one outdoor performance where the plan was to sneak them out to the car—which was parked a quarter of a mile away—by a small-gauge railroad. The only problem was that the train moved so slowly that even fans who were walking outpaced it and were waiting by their car! It was mad, totally ridiculous, and they couldn't help but laugh.

They were on their way to play a roadshow in Nottingham, England, when the band received a phone call. Their management had received word that when the new chart came out, "Bring It All Back" would be number one. If they'd screamed and shouted before, that was nothing on this. They were hugging each other and yelling. Anticipating the event, their managers had put a bottle of champagne in the minibus, and so they pulled off and toasted success—after which each of them pulled out their mobile phones and began calling family and friends to pass on the good news.

When they ran onto the stage in Nottingham, the announcer let the audience in on the chart secret—and the band had to act as if they didn't already know (and they did a very good job of it). From there it was a mad dash down to London, to appear on Capital FM's chart countdown show. There they had a chance to talk about themselves, their experiences, and what it felt like to be at the top. Over the course of that weekend alone they sold a staggering 90,000 copies of the single, a pretty remarkable feat. That was amazing, but it couldn't compete with performing live on *Top of the Pops*. That really was the ultimate for all of them, to be up onstage in front of an audience, going out all over the country, knowing they were number one. How could you top something like that?

Not easily is the answer, but it's also the kind of boost that can keep you going for a long time. In the wake of being, quite literally, top of the pops, there were more and more shows organized, although they were still only in Britain.

And all the guys and girls had to come to terms with the idea of being stars, because that was exactly what they'd become. Between television and the charts, they were big, there was no two ways about it. They were recognized and mobbed by fans wherever they went. It was the kind of thing no one can prepare for, but still gratifying, even while a little scary.

The biggest deal to come out of it was when they were asked to play Party In The Park, a huge outdoor show in London's Hyde Park, put on by the Prince's Trust, the charity formed by Charles, Prince of Wales (who would be in attendance). That was a compliment and an honor. But it was also terrifying.

By now Rachel, Jon, Hannah, Bradley, Tina, Paul, and Jo were used to performing in front of crowds. But 100,000 people qualified as more than a crowd. To say they were nervous before they went on was putting it mildly. But they were troupers, real professionals, so they bounced onto the stage and gave it their all, even thought most of the audience could only see them because of the giant monitors. They sang "Bring It All Back," and then it was over. Backstage, they looked as they'd been hit by a truck, they were all so dazed. The energy, they all agreed, had been totally overwhelming. Not just the energy they received from the crowd, but what they'd put out, too. It left them all exhausted. For Jo, in particular, it was a highlight of her singing career; never had she felt anything like that. All they could do was sit and wait to recover. For three minutes they'd really given their all, and it had drained them. But in a good cause, and on a day to remember.

The bond between the Club members kept them going a lot of the time. If someone was down, the others could cheer him or her up. And by having so many people— you think of another band with seven singers—they avoided the little cliques that could sometimes happen, and kept things on a very even keel. They were in this to work, because what had started out as a job had become something they loved, and none of them ever forgot that.

CHAPTER FOUR

YOU'VE HAD one big hit . . . the only way to beat that is to have another, and that was exactly what the Club hoped to do, to prove they was much more than a fluke, and that they were here to stay. Of the material they'd recorded, several tracks stood as good possibilities, but possibly the most commercial was "S Club Party." Not only was it a great song, but it said a lot about who they were, just in case people didn't already know.

It's true that every single these days needs a video. Given that the song was about having fun, about life being a party, a video with plenty of dancing made perfect sense—especially since the Club's performances were all nonstop singing and dancing, anyway. The question was, where should they shoot it?

America was the perfect answer. Thanks to the show, the Club were very definitely associated with the States. This time, however, it wouldn't be in Florida, but out West, in California. *That*, too, made perfect sense, since the Club were heading there to film a television special.

The location chosen for the video was Vasquez Rocks (and for the special), in the desert outside Los Angeles. Plenty of films had done location shooting there, including *Star Trek*, it was accessible, but still looked relatively barren, while still decidedly American.

The main prop was a collection of fifties classic cars (something that popped up in the series, this video, and in their special. . . . ongoing theme, anyone?)—something uniquely American, and utterly beautiful, the kind of thing everyone would love to own, or at least drive. Apart from that, it was the Club themselves who provided the visual entertainment with their choreography.

Like any video shoot, it was hard work, and it was boring. The desert sun was, if anything, hotter than they'd known in Florida, and left them dehydrated and exhausted. The day was long, too, running through the tune endless times, performing the dances. But the end product was more than worth the effort. Over the course of a two-day shoot, they completed the video. When the band seems to make the magical *S* while up in the air, they were actually bouncing on a trampoline. If you watch closely, you'll see Jo's jump isn't as good as the others, more as if she was falling—which was exactly what she was doing.

Once again they were filming, and once again, that meant very little rest, although by now that seemed to be the norm, not the exception. However, if they'd thought they had to get up early in Florida, they had a major shock coming. Their wake-up calls there had been five-thirty or six. In Los Angeles they sometimes had to rise at two-thirty or three in the morning, not the most pleasant hour by *anyone's* standards. They all suffered from that, not only Bradley. But by now they were so used to the waking routine that it came without thought, and they were ready to hit hair and makeup in twenty minutes. And they could do it without complaining. For the next twelve days, they were going to be very busy indeed

The special was for British television, and was to be called *Back to the Fifties*, a tribute to, and celebration of, America in the 1950s, when sock hops were where kids danced, malt shops and drive-in movies were where you took a date, and rock 'n' roll was still a very new thing. It was an era the members of the Club had all missed by more than two and a half decades, but it was one that had lived on in shows like *Happy Days* as a more innocent, fun time.

And it had produced some enduring music and movies. People like Elvis Presley and James Dean were the big stars of the time, and their images live on. *Back to the Fifties* would be a minimovie of sorts, and would actually be shown—once—in a movie theater in London, for its official premiere, which would coincide with a concert by the band.

The special itself had the Club driving into a small American town, and being in a kind of fifties time warp, with four of them ending up briefly in jail. There were shades of movies like *Jailhouse Rock* and *Rebel Without a Cause*, all lovingly done. However, said Tina, "The car kept breaking down every few seconds. That good old Chevy wasn't that good at all. And we had a stunt man to do some stunts with the car, but somebody forgot to buy tubes to put into the tires which makes it safe for stunts, so he couldn't do anything with the car."

But even with a car that couldn't really perform, they got through everything okay. The days were long—on a few occasions they worked for sixteen or seventeen hours straight—but there was so much to do. They'd only received the scripts a couple of days before filming began, so there were lines to learn, scenes to be blocked, as well as some choreography to take in. It meant an awful lot was demanded of them, and success was resting on their shoulders. But, as the end result showed, they came through perfectly. By the time the premiere rolled around, they had plenty to be proud of.

That was quite an event, and one that was bigger than anyone had expected. Literally thousands of fans were lined up outside the Odeon in Leicester Square, trying to get in to the show. The band, meanwhile, were in a hotel across the street, watching everything that was going on.

"That was a really amazing feeling," recalled Rachel. "I felt a bit choked!"

They made their entrance in (what else!) a classic American car, driving up to the theater—not exactly a long drive—but arriving in perfect style. But, being S Club, they couldn't have everything too formal. The Odeon was an old, old theater. Its history went back to the days of silent films, when an organist used to accompany the action, playing live. That meant there was an organ pit, which was now empty, and the band decided to rise up through that. It was dramatic, and against a black stage, adorned with only a red S Club 7 logo, very, very effective. It added to the whole feel of the performance, and gave them another buzz from the performing, in front of a group of fans who'd come out just to see *them*. For Paul, in particular, this was the best gig they'd played so far, a night to be remembered and treasured forever. But for all of them it was a total blast, one more great thing in a career that simply seemed to get better and better. And once it was over they were escorted to their seats to enjoy the film.

Once the movie itself had aired, there was also a reel of outtakes, just to show how human they were. It included a wonderful scene of Jo with mud stuck in her mouth, unable to say her lines, and another where Paul flicked oatmeal onto someone's shoe, which made a totally disgusting noise. It had everyone in stitches—band and audience alike.

It coincided with the release of their second single, "S Club Party." In a lot of ways, this was more important than "Bring It All Back," because it would show whether they were one-hit wonders, or whether they really had made it all the way to the big time.

From the time of its release, it became apparent that "S Club Party" was going to follow in the footsteps of "Bring It All Back." The record exploded onto the charts and began climbing rapidly. But could it go all the way to number one? Could they manage that twice in a row?

It seemed like Tina, Paul, Hannah, Jon, Rachel, Bradley, and Tina were everywhere in Britain. They popped up on morning television, on every possible show, made appearances all over the country. Magazines could hardly get enough of them. And then, of course, there was the chance to appear on *Top of the Pops* again, which they relished. MTV in Britain was showing the video in heavy rotation. Things couldn't have been better.

Well, they could, actually. . . . and they got a whole lot better when the single did climb to the number one position. Now no one could say S Club 7 was just a flash in the pan. They'd really established themselves among the hitmakers of 1999 in Britain. It was a total thrill for everyone to have this happen, and to say they were psyched when they heard the news would be putting it mildly. Nothing might compare with the news of a first number one record . . . but a second came very, very close indeed.

Not since the Monkees had any band been stars of both a television show and on the pop charts. The double-pronged attack was a natural fit, however. Television was pop culture, and went hand in hand with music, especially since the advent of music videos. S Club 7 simply married the two ideas in brilliant fashion—the main surprise was that no one else had done since the 1960s, really.

But it worked because of a lot of talent, and a lot of hard work on everyone's part. The Club might have been a manufactured group originally, but all that had done was to get them started. From there, the chemistry between the seven of them was what had made it all work, and turned it into some real magic. Their personalities were what put the show across, even more than the writing, and that crossed over into the music. Yes, it was all very cleverly marketed, and that helped, but what really made S Club a success was the people in it, who were giving it their all, 24/7.

Even as they were celebrating their new hit, there was plenty going on in S World. They jetted off to San Francisco for a couple of days, to promote the series, which would soon be reaching American viewers—it was already showing in Australia, New Zealand, and several other countries—before heading off Down Under for more promotion there. Their album was almost ready for release in the UK. Soon they'd be heading off to the studio to begin work on their *next* album, and after that they'd be back in Los Angeles to make a Christmas special for British television. Once all that was done, would they have a break? Of course . . . not!

But first there was the small matter of the album, wasn't there?

It was called *S Club*, and it was eleven tracks of pure fun. To those who'd seen the series and the special, there was nothing new, but it was finally here in a form everyone could keep. Both the singles were on there—and there was nothing wrong with that—but the other nine tracks were every bit as good. They covered the range from slinky, R&B-tipped ballads, to out-and-out dance music, and every single one of them could have been a major pop smash.

It started off, as anything to do with the Club should, with their theme song, "Bring It All Back," as bouncy and positive a piece of pop as anyone was likely to find, and a real manifesto for what S Club 7 was all about. If you believed in yourself, you could do anything. It had everything a pop song needed, with a powerful chorus, great hooks, and a wonderful dance routine (as everyone who caught the video knows). The fact that people had heard it so often on the show made it familiar, and its number one status was a strong way to start off the record.

From there it was into "You're My Number One," which, with the following track, "Two In A Million," would become S Club's third single, close to Christmas. "You're My Number One" was something of throwback to the seventies, with shades of glam rock and Abba, midtempo, and great structure, with a slinky chorus that used all the voices to great effect. It was possibly even more catchy than their first two singles, without ever being stupid. It was, simply, just great pop music. And, on top of all that, it had a fab singalong quality—it was impossible to resist, as record buyers in the UK discovered.

"Two In A Million" slowed things down a lot, working on that Motown-R&B area. Again, it was great songwriting, with some clever arrangements that took a few slightly unexpected turns—but not too unexpected. It was made for dancing close with someone you cared about, but there was still enough personality in it to make it seem very definitely S Club, unlike so much of the anonymous R&B that seemed to be released. And it showed that the Club could be just as effective when the lights dimmed.

"S Club Party" had been their second number one in Britain, and it was easy to see why. It was as infectious as a cold, but tons more fun. There was plenty of hip-hop in the mix, along with dance music. Not a frantic groove, still laid-back enough, but it would get you sweating out on the dance floor. Jo's lead vocals showed her voice in full effect, but always it was the others in support that filled out the sound. And it really introduced all the members—and in the video there was some great breakdancing from Paul, showing some moves no one suspected he had. It was exactly what it was meant to be, a great party record, and it was easy to see why it had been such a big success.

From there came "Everybody Wants Ya," one of the most memorable songs from the show. It was straight ahead pop music with lots of seventies overtones, even a touch of disco. It underlined the care that had gone into this band. They could have just slapped the album together, but instead there was a lot of thought in every aspect, and the songs were all world-class. Here it was the chorus that was like Velcro, sticking to the mind and impossible to remove. It made you want to be part of it, singing and dancing along, and that was what the Club really meant—being part of the party.

"Viva La Fiesta" was a tip to the way Latin music had become so hot during 1999. It might not have been quite as authentic as Ricky Martin, but that hardly mattered. It had that Cuban groove that got the hips shaking. There were loads of percussion to propel the salsa, and the kind of chorus that really did make you want to throw your hands in the air. It was quite relentless, and the rhythm definitely took control. It was a dance song, nothing more or less, but it certainly succeeded!

After that came "Gonna Change The World," which was a big title for a slow song, one that featured Bradley's vocals, and gave the other boys a chance to show what they could do, too. After hearing so much of the girls, it made for a nice change, and to hear the guys do a tender love song was more than nice. It was the kind of slow jam everyone needs once in a while, especially if you're in love, when you really believe your love *can* change the world. And after "Viva La Fiesta," things really needed to chill a little bit.

"I Really Miss You" was something else slow, and the girls' outing, with more than a hint of seventies soul—although with more bass. It was something to give the Spice Girls a run for their money, or any of the girls who had appeared in their wake. Giving each of the genders a workout was a good idea. Not only did it add some variety to the mix, but it proved that everyone was supertalented, and capable of doing great things.

But after that it was time to crank up the energy again—after all, you can't have a party that doesn't get crazy, and "Friday Night" was the ideal song for that. It was a favorite of most of the band, and it was easy to see why. Starting with scratching, it hit a deep, funky groove very quickly, with Bradley rapping—a talent he'd kept quiet, but shouldn't have. And when he started singing, he showed once more how soulful his voice was. Even if you were sitting, it was impossible to remain still when this was playing. But Friday night was the night to party, after all, with school out, and the weekend ahead. Nothing was more likely to get you in that mood than this jam. It had everything going, everyone working vocally off each other in some complex arrangements—a sort of S Club trademark—that were so smooth you never even realized how difficult they were to achieve. A top track.

"It's A Feel Good Thing" was exactly that, another venture into Latin music, but one with a dance music feel, as the bass drum kept four to the floor. It even had some Spanish lyrics, and kept exploding higher and higher with each chorus. The energy on it was unbelievable, even more than on the other uptempo tracks, with everyone giving it their all, partying on the song like tomorrow would never come—and maybe it never would, if you kept playing it over and over.

It all wound down with "Hope For The Future," which once again featured Jo and Bradley's vocals, and kicked things out by chilling a little on something softer to close. It was the song featured on the show with the dolphins, and was memorable for that alone, but it also happened to be a killer R&B song. And it ended things on a very positive note, too.

All in all, *S Club* was as strong a debut as anyone had ever put out. It proved that the Club really stood out from the pack of teen bands. Their personalities came across, even on CD. There was a strong variety of songs, all great pop music, well arranged, and carefully recorded. At the same time, while it was smooth, it wasn't overproduced. You could still sense the very human touches behind it all.

Jo and Bradley carried most of the lead vocals (but certainly not all), and it was impossible to deny that they both had great voices, the kind that really made you sit up and take notice. Both of them could belt it out and also be more sensitive, and Bradley in particular had a very soulful quality to his singing.

Given how good it was, and how popular the club was, it was no surprise that it shot into the British album charts at number two. If anything, the surprise was that it didn't enter at number one—but it would quickly capture that spot. That was yet another thrill to add to the many they'd experienced this year—it never seemed to stop, and why should it?

The thing was, they weren't even home to enjoy the pleasure of reading the music papers and seeing their album hit the top. As always, they were incredibly busy, bouncing all over the world. They were back in America again, filming the video for what would be their third single,. and also making yet another special called *Boyfriends and Birthdays*, which was set to air in the UK a couple of weeks before Christmas—their Christmas present to the fans who'd treated them so well. Being a member of S Club meant never slowing down—and not getting much chance to sleep, either.

With a hit series, two top singles and a top album, they'd already achieved so much in a few months. It truly was like a dream come true, from nowhere to utter stars in such a short time. But even though they were all exhausted, the excitement of it kept them going . . . and going . . . and going.

CHAPTER FIVE

S CLUB 7 in Miami premiered on American television screens without a great deal of hype and fanfare. It was just another new series starting in the fall season on the Fox Family Channel. The Club might have been massive in Britain, but in the States they were just part of another show. When it was first shown, no one even really knew they were a proper band with chart hits and real pop credentials.

America was actually one of forty-three countries to be showing the series, but because of its sheer size, it was one of the very major markets. And, of course, everyone was more than happy to go over and promote the show. They'd done a couple of days of that in San Francisco, and now they returned to America, this time to New York, to do even more. Obviously, it was in their own interests, but they also loved America because, Paul said, "No one notices us. We're well-known in most other countries except America, so when we go there we really are normal."

What was interesting was the way viewers found the show. It was mostly by word of mouth, though friends at school. The charts in the fall of 1999 were dominated by names like the Backstreet Boys, Britney Spears, Christina Aguilera, and a few others—all homegrown,

American talent. No British bands were getting a look-at.

It became apparent that might soon change when, on the weekend after Thanksgiving, Fox Family decided to run a marathon of *Miami* episodes. The ratings had been increasing, but they weren't through the roof—yet. And viewers didn't know that "Bring It All Back" was actually out in the States as a single—there'd been no real publicity or ads to that effect. And if you don't know something's available, getting it becomes that much harder.

During the marathon, the band's American label, Interscope, had an ad with a toll-free number. Viewers could call and get a free S Club 7 record. According to the label, they'd expected in the region of 20,000 calls. They'd have been satisfied with that figure as a starting point for the band. Instead they received a total of *seven million* calls—something totally unprecedented, and enough to bring down their entire phone system for a while. Somewhere out there, S Club 7 was building a huge American fan base, quietly and gradually. On the strength of the response, Interscope decided to bring forward the release of *S Club* from Spring 2000 to January, realizing they might well have something very major on their hands.

It wouldn't be the only marathon of the show that Fox Family would run—there'd be another at New Year, and a third on Super Bowl Sunday—but it was the only time Interscope made their offer! And the show stuck in its regular Saturday morning slot, offering a great alternative to cartoons, and getting more and more people viewing. If it took a while to find its audience, that was fine; there was time. The series could be repeated and no one would mind. While there was an ongoing story, virtually each episode also stood alone.

There wasn't too much time for the Club to promote the show in America. Their time was controlled almost to the minute.

"I remember when management used to say, 'It's gonna get really busy soon, once it all starts you won't believe how it will take off,' " said Hannah. "When it hit, we were working every day, bang, bang, bang."

After a summer of playing shows, they'd really gotten back in the swing with the Christmas special filming in Los Angeles, and the video shoots for "You're My Number One" and "Two In A Million." They'd had twelve days for the special, and there were two more days for the "Two In A Million" video, which saw the girls with a new look. Tina, Jo, and Rachel all wore hair extensions, while Hannah had hers heavily gelled and twisted.

It was an especially grueling shoot.

"The first day we got there at six in the morning, and worked until half nine in the evening, which is a long day," recalled Bradley. "The second day was from twelve o'clock in the afternoon till five in the morning!" It's just as well they've all got a lot of natural energy—they need it.

From there it was off to Australia and New Zealand for promotion. The girls went shopping. Hannah—who'd been there before to visit relatives—led the girls on a shopping trip—of course!—and the Club engaged in a volleyball game against a professional team on Sydney's famous Bondi Beach—a good way to make work seem like play. And they had been given professional instruction themselves, back in Florida.

Before they traveled to the States or Australia, though, they'd been very busy in the recording studio, starting work on their second album. They managed to complete six tracks, including Hannah's favorite, "Reach For The Stars," which gave Jo some problems.

"Jo was really, really sick . . . and she had to go into the studio to record the song 'Reach For The Stars,' " said Jon. "That's tough 'cause you feel like you're not giving your best."

Interestingly, among the material recorded were solo tracks by each of the Club, giving them a chance to shine individually. As soon as they returned from the lands Down Under, they were whisked back into the studio to complete their vocal work on the new record prior to Christmas 1999. There was definitely no rest for the wicked, and never enough time to be truly wicked, either.

You'd think that they might have been allowed some time off over the holidays—and they were. There was a two week break over Christmas and New Year, which they all desperately needed. But if you'd been in Britain, you'd have thought they were working away. *Boyfriends and Birthdays* aired on television there in December, and the double-sided single "You're My Number One/Two In A Million" appeared the day after the show had been on television, making it a candidate for the coveted Christmas number one position.

In Britain, having the Christmas number one is a very big deal. It receives a huge amount of publicity, and in 1999 it was going to be quite a battle. Apart from S Club 7, top bands like Westlife, Steps, and B*witched would have singles out, as well as the venerable Sir Cliff Richard, a pop institution since the 1950s, with his song "The Millennium Prayer." There was also a charity record, where stars had gotten together on a number whose profits would benefit the charity Children's Promise. The song was the Rolling Stones' "It's Only Rock 'n' Roll," and included contributions from the Spice Girls, Kid Rock, Mick Jagger, Mary J. Blige, Natalie Imbruglia, Dolores of the Cranberries, Jay Kay of Jamiroquoi, Gavin Rossdale of Bush, Iggy Pop, Status Quo, comedian Eric Idle (of Monty Python fame)—and S Club 7. That one didn't reach the top. But neither did S Club's own single, losing out to Cliff over both Christmas and the millennium week.

But fans who bought the S Club 7 single did get a couple of bonuses on the disc. There was a nonalbum track, "Down at Club S," which had been featured in the *Chevy* episode of the series, but never before released, and there was also the video of "You're My Number

One," which was made on the run while they'd been filming *Back to the Fifties*. Set in a bowling alley, it featured them bowling (or in Tina's case, throwing gutter balls, while Jo's went flying into the air—Hannah couldn't even lift the ball), dancing (some very impressive flips down the lane by Jon), and generally enjoying themselves eating hot dogs, while other members of the cast from the special danced to the song in the background. It was fun, it had the feel of a home movie, and it had been shot without too much extra work on the part of the band—which was probably a big plus for them.

"Down at Club S" was a real treasure. It was primarily dance-pop, but around the edges it had a lot of a Latin beat, especially on the chorus. If "Bring It All Back" hadn't been so great, this could easily have been their theme song, detailing how inclusive they were, and how they wanted *everyone* to be a part of the Club and enjoy themselves. It grooved very merrily along, completely catchy and bouncy, and it was so good you had to seriously wonder why it had been left off the album (answer: so it could be a bonus cut on a single like this!). There were a few other songs from the series that hadn't made it onto the album, too—"So Right," which had been featured in the *Alligator* episode (which had actually also appeared on their first single), "We Can Work It Out," as well as their cover tunes—Tony Orlando's "Tie A Yellow Ribbon," Carly Simon's "Nobody Does It Better," and their completely unforgettable take on Abba's "Dancing Queen." Maybe sometime those will see the light of day.

Over the Christmas break, everyone in the band had a chance to catch up with their families. For Hannah, in particular, that was welcome. She'd missed her family and friends, and headed back to Great Yarmouth to celebrate.

"I always go out with my mates on Christmas Eve and I can't wait 'cause we get all dressed up and put wigs on and have a mad night."

The day itself would be spent with family, and going over everything that had been achieved during the year— as well as looking forward to everything that was ahead. And there was also the chance to watch the Christmas edition of *Top of the Pops*, which would give her the opportunity to see herself twice. And, of course, there were presents to open, including gifts all the members of the Club had given each other. Paul was considering buying shoes for Tina (like she didn't already have enough!), some trainers for Jo, and, of course, beauty products for Rachel. But, in reality, their plan was to buy each other novelty, gag gifts "and when we open them we laugh for about an hour," said Jon.

For all of them, the break was very necessary. They'd been going full tilt for over a year now, with just little bits of time off here and there, but no real vacation, even as the workload became greater and greater. And from the look of things, 2000 looked to be even busier! It would have been easy to think of them burning out, but they were determined that wouldn't happen.

"The more exhausted you feel, the more you're aware of the hard work and sometimes you really have to remind yourself that you're doing a lot of cool things," pointed out Tina. They were, perhaps, learning how to pace themselves a little, instead of rushing headlong into everything, and leaving a bit of their energy for later, difficult as that might be. The last twelve months had been pretty overwhelming, but now, with a little perspective, they could see how things were going, and how to be able to manage everything that was expected of them.

The most immediate thing on the horizon was the filming of the next S Club 7 series, once again in America. That would happen in the new year. At least this time they wouldn't be quite as rushed as they had been in Miami. Instead of having eight weeks to film thirteen episodes, this time they'd have the luxury of a whopping eleven weeks—woohoo!

Actually, it would be the longest single stretch most of them had been gone, especially Rachel and Jo, for whom it meant leaving their boyfriends. But they were really learning how to cope. When the stress became too much, they'd just go out on a shopping spree, or have a party, something to blow it all away, no matter how stupid it might seem. They all still had their sense of humor (and sense of awe) about it all. And they'd all learned that eating right really helped too—maintaining a good diet for the energy it could bring. No matter how busy they were, there was always the time to have a meal so they could carry on—it was vitally important.

By the time the Club arrived back in the States to begin filming the second series of the show, quite a lot of people knew who they were. It wasn't like England where Jo went to see her nephew at his school sports day, "and I couldn't even watch him run, 'cause there were hundreds of kids after me." But enough people had seen the show to make them recognizable figures to quite a few of the population.

They hadn't even been famous for twelve months yet, but they'd crammed so much into a year, and yet it was only a part of what they might be able to achieve. There was a great deal planned for the year 2000, including at tour of Britain, and maybe other parts of the world (if time allowed). Britain made sense, since they were established pop stars there, and while they'd done roadshow gigs, there had never been a real tour, where they were headlining.

One thing was for certain. If they thought they'd been under pressure before, it was nothing compared to what they'd be facing now. It had all gone totally mad. Granted, they knew exactly what they'd be doing until March, but after that it was really going to get crazy. But, as Jon said, "We'll put the work in, we'll give it everything we've got." A lot was asked of them, but they had an awful lot to give.

Having broken massively in Britain, and having established a fan base in plenty of other countries, thanks to the show, they could now concentrate on being taken seriously as a band in those other countries. Places like America, Canada, Australia, and New Zealand seemed natural fits for their music, with a love of good pop. And with so much music aimed at teens making the charts, there was absolutely no reason why S Club 7 couldn't be huge everywhere, the way BSB or Britney had become.

It says a lot that Rachel, Paul, Jo, Bradley, Hannah, Jon, and Tina don't think of themselves as stars, but as ordinary people. "Your brain can't comprehend it," said Jo, "but every now and then you sit down and take a reality check." Perhaps it's because it's happened so quickly, or because they spent so much of 1999 out of Britain, that they haven't really seen just how it all blew up for them there, the way it will in other countries during 2000. Or, more likely, because they simply are ordinary people, regular people, who aren't the type to put on airs simply because they are stars.

Inevitably, though, there have been a few changes.

"You notice how people change around you and it opens your eyes to see who your mates really are," noted Hannah. "I don't think we've changed toward people at all, it's actually people around us that have changed."

That's inevitably what happens, though, when people get famous. People they'd been at school with, casual acquaintances all want to be best friends, and suddenly you have to be very wary of everyone new.

At least Jo and Rachel had their boyfriends, whom they'd known since before all this began, and they could be sure of them. But, in turn, their fame put a strain on the relationship. With them gone so much, and so many demands on their time even when they were home, it was hard to have a real relationship.

Everyone thinks that for bands, most of their time is spent performing. But once you're famous, that's actually not true.

"There's a lot more photo shoots and interviews than I expected," pointed out Hannah. "Not much of it is actually performing."

You might think that because they were stars, all the members of S Club 7 were rich. That was still very far from the truth. They were doing nicely, it was true, but they definitely weren't what anyone could consider rich. None of them had the money to go out and buy a house, or even to buy a car. They were all in the Club because it was great fun.

"For me it's the pure satisfaction you get once you see the end product of your hard work," said Hannah. And there was a huge satisfaction in watching a video you'd spent two days working on and sweating to complete, or seeing your record in the charts, or watching your show on television. At that point you had something real to show for all the effort you'd put into it.

Being so busy, and being so famous, also meant that you learned to treasure the things that were really important, like family and true friends. For all of them, when they had a break, it meant spending time with family and mates, where you could still be yourself and just relax. Without feeling you had to be on show. It was a chance for a laugh, and also to be pampered a bit. And after all those trips, that was important. When they were traveling, all too often they weren't in one place long enough to even unpack. They'd learned how to live out of suitcases, to think ahead for what clothes they'd need. At home they could stretch out and have their own things around them, which had to seem like a real luxury. They could play their music, or just enjoy the silence, and relish actually having some space around them. It was great to be one of the Club, but at times it was good to be alone, too—that was one of the reasons they no longer shared hotel rooms. Everyone needs some space and privacy in their lives.

It was a real mark of how far the Club had come, and how quickly, that they could have two specials on British television in just a matter of months. First, with *Back to the Fifties*, and then with *Boyfriends and Birthdays*. On top of that, the latter was aired just a couple of weeks before Christmas, which made it really prime time viewing. Then there was also the release of their first home video (and in all likelihood there will be others), *It's an S Club Thing*.

Unlike many home videos, this was much more than a series of music videos. It got to grips with all seven of the people, had them talking quite freely about their experiences, how they ended up in the band, and there was even footage of some early rehearsals! In fact, the only music video on the whole tape was for "S Club Party." There was also not a huge amount about *S Club 7 in Miami*, mostly because anyone who'd seen the series (and read *S Club 7 in Miami: The Official Scrapbook*) had a pretty good idea what had happened there. It was a home video issued only in the UK—which made a great deal of sense. That was where they'd been successful, and had the hit singles they discussed, where they'd performed, and where the audience had seen the *Back to the Fifties* special. To other viewers, a lot of it would make no sense at all.

One thing it definitely wasn't was a ripoff. You came away with a very good sense of what made Tina, Jon, Rachel, Bradley, Jo, Paul, and Hannah tick, why they were doing this, and what they'd done before they became members of the Club. In other words, instead of stars, they came across as very real, flesh-and-blood human beings, people with pasts, and hopes, and dreams— as well as being a group that loved a good laugh. You could see them celebrating and you could see them tired. Indeed, some of the footage was shot by band members themselves, giving it a very intimate feel.

Everything acted as a great cap to a remarkable year. From obscurity to fame and fortune in one giant leap. The TV show, the specials, the hit singles the hit album, and even being asked to participate in a very high-profile charity record—it was the type of thing everyone dreams about. There was no doubt that S Club 7 had really found their audience with kids, and a place in their collective hearts.

And that was why it was full marks to them for also becoming involved in a couple of campaigns. They didn't need to be. They could have just been stars, but instead they were intent on giving something back.

One involvement was with the World Wildlife Fund, which was dedicated to preserving animals around the globe. A lot of species are endangered, and the Fund collects money to be able to keep those species going, to keep habitats intact, and help the entire world ecosystem. It might not have been the hippest cause around, but the Club were more than happy to lend their names to it, adopting animals, and making people aware of the work the WWF was doing. As part of that, they were present at Whipsnade Zoo, not far from London, in October 1999, for a World Wildlife Fund day, being photographed with various animals, and doing what they could to raise the awareness of both the plight and the need for help. Things like this were vitally important, not only for the animals themselves, but also for the future of the planet, and everyone was glad to be a part of it.

The other involvement had begun earlier in the year, back in June, when S Club 7 helped launch Woolworth's Kids First, an umbrella charity aimed at raising funds to help kids and distribute money to other charities. Its main purpose, really, was to help stop bullying in schools, something that's always been a problem around the world, but which definitely has to stop! Over the years far too many kids had suffered from it. While none of the Club themselves had really suffered from it, having grown up, they were aware, as everyone is, that it existed, and how bad it could really be. Anything that helped improve things had to be a positive step, and to lend their name and image to it—especially since their biggest fans were kids—would help. Again, it was based in Britain, but that was the band's home, after all, and a place where they were massive and really could help make a difference.

But things like this, and taking the time to sign autographs after performances, which they've always done, showed that there was a lot more to them than people on television or on a CD. They cared about the world they lived in and about the people who supported them. It was all well and good being a star, but if you didn't try and improve your world, then the fame ended up being rather hollow—which was something they'd realized early on. Over the coming years, there will doubtless be plenty of other charitable involvements as the band just becomes bigger and bigger. But that's the way it should be. They have names, and they're more than happy to lend them to a good cause. Really, it helps inspire others, too, and adds to one of the band's philosophies: "Nothing is impossible. We can do it." And that's quite true. By banding together, people can truly make a difference.

CHAPTER SIX

IF 1999 seemed busy for everyone in the Club, the year 2000 will seem like a madhouse. They are, really, the band that typifies the new millennium—fun, funky, funny, and fabulous. But they're also made up of people who look and dress like real people. None of the girls, even though they're babes, will try to pass as a supermodel or a half-clothed sex symbol. None of the guys is going to be mistaken for a movie star. That's part of the beauty of it; they're really not trying to be something they aren't, just seven people who are having great fun together, and have talent in several different areas. It's unlikely you'll find them at top fashion shows anywhere (okay, maybe Rachel). And it's unlikely you'll ever see them onstage wearing big designer names. Their image is casual, the girls wearing the baby tops and jeans, sport pants, or capris, the boys in tees, sweatshirts, or open-neck shirts. It's a style, of course, and one that suits them, in that it reflects exactly what so many of their fans are wearing. It helps to make the Club inclusive, not exclusive.

Their appeal, though, does go beyond kids. They're a band parents can like. Their pop has many seventies touches, all too familiar to parents from their youth. And all seven come across as regular people, always ready for a laugh, but clean and wholesome. In an S Club 7 dance routine you won't find the guys grabbing at their crotches to make a point—there's no overt sexuality involved at all. In other words, they're the pop band parents can feel good about their kids liking. And to have something parents and kids can agree on makes for a very pleasant change.

Having conquered Britain in 1999, 2000 is when they can set their gaze on the rest of the world. In so many countries the series has introduced them to a generation and brought them fans. Now, as their album is released, and people become aware that it's out there, they can build on that fan base and become real stars. It won't be easy, or automatic. There's going to be a lot of hard work involved in translating television success to a place at the top of the charts around the globe. But as they've all too clearly shown, Rachel, Jon, Hannah, Paul, Jo, Bradley, and Tina are not afraid of a lot of hard work—in fact, it's become the norm for them.

But, although their sights are set on the world, they won't be forgetting their home base. Britain will be getting a new S Club album and series before anyone else— which is enough to make a lot of people in other countries very jealous. They'll also get the pleasure of an S Club 7 tour in the summer. However, if they're really big elsewhere, there might be more than one country involved in that tour. That remains up in the air, however, and will also depend, in large part, upon their schedule, which becomes more and more crammed as the days go by.

That's the way it goes, though. But in between all the travel and the lack of sleep, there's also the chance to keep making dreams come true, like swimming with the dolphins, seeing so many countries, and doing all kinds of shopping. While there are downsides, it's really a great life, and they know it. They're lucky, and that's something they understand all too well. Out of the hundreds that applied to be charter members of the Club, they're the seven who made it, who had the right talents to make it all work. It could easily have been someone else. Still, as Bradley pointed out, it's probably a good thing they're usually so busy that they don't know up from down, because "if it wasn't busy we'd be getting worried."

But there's no danger of that happening for the foreseeable future. They've become a juggernaut, one that seems impossible to stop. In a few short months they've achieved so much—just imagine what it'll be like in a couple more years!

Their second album will be one to give them the chance to explore things a bit more, musically. It still won't really stay far from pop, but it will offer each of them the chance to show their individual talents, apart from a band. And then, as the band, they've had the time to really gel and develop a full-on personality now. So while it won't be so different as to turn off all the people who bought the first record, it will almost certainly cover a wider range of material. And there's nothing wrong with that.

If you want to look at it, there are a few parallels with the music of the Spice Girls (and not just because they had the same management). On their first album, the Girls played it very straight with some excellent danceable pop and ballads. On their second album, they really broadened things a lot, even including some Latin music—and that was before it hit big worldwide. Now, of course, the Club have Latin influence on a couple of their songs, but where will they go musically in the future?

That has yet to be figured out. Certainly a lot of the music from this new album will be on the second series of the show, just as the first gave everyone a chance to hear all the material on their debut. But that's perfect— and exactly the way the Monkees did it in the mid-sixties. More than three decades on and nothing has changed at all! But in a way, that's rather comforting, to show that a few things remain constant in a world whose face seems to alter almost daily.

Most likely, the second season of S Club 7 on television won't change too much. The characters have been established, and since they work so well (and, for the most part, are close to who the Club really are), there's no reason to change them. And this time around, with all their experience, none of them will be tentative in the first few episodes, the way Jo and a couple of the others were in the first season. So it will be more dynamic, explosive—and maybe even funnier, if such a thing is possible.

And, believe it or not, it makes sense for them to hold off on touring until the summer. For a start, there's been no time before for a real tour. But there was also the fact that they didn't have enough material to tour as headliners. What they did have were the songs from the first album, and a couple more from the show. By summer 2000, with two albums' worth of material to choose from, plus a few more songs from the show, they'll be able to present a really exciting, nonstop show on the stage, a real spectacle of music and dance.

In between now and then, though, there'll be plenty of hard work. By now they'll probably be wrapping up work on the second series—which means that once again Paul will celebrate his birthday far from home. Then, as soon as they're home, the new series will probably begin airing, and there'll be a new single to go out and promote, as well as a million other things to fill their time. And they'll have to start rehearsing for the tour. There'll also be promotion in other parts of the world, including the big push in America. They'll be lucky if they know what country they're in, let alone what day it is!

So is there a danger of burnout? Can they all be asked to do just too much in too short a time? It's a question that's occurred to all of them, really, and it would be impossible for it not to come up. The year 1999 was stressful, but in part that was because it was all so new. The pace was hectic, but these days they're much more used to it. That doesn't mean there won't be problems, of course, but at least they know what they're dealing with, and they each have their little ways of coping—like giving each other space, or all getting totally mad together to blow off the steam. They've never stopped and talked to each other about what it's like to be famous, and the pressures that come with it, however. For a start, it's not the English way to discuss your feelings, but also, deep down, none of them feels famous. They're simply the same people they always were.

Of course, once you start believing you're famous, start believing the stuff the press writes about you, everything changes. You can't see yourself as the same person any more. But with seven of them around, there's no danger of any one getting a swelled head in this Club. They make sure each other's feet stay very firmly planted on the ground.

In Britain, the tabloids have featured them, of course. They're well known, so they're news. But none of them has any scandal, and even the supposed "battle" between them and the band Steps, so hyped by a couple of the daily papers, never existed. In fact, the two bands know and like each other, and there has *never* been a problem between them.

At the beginning of 1999, the first articles about the Club were appearing in the American teen magazines, which tended to be about three months behind what was actually happening. *Teen Beat* interviewed Tina, Jon, Rachel, Paul, Jo, Bradley, and Hannah, but it was a certainty that would just be the start, as their star was rising. Within four days of the S Club album being released in America on January 25, Amazon.com was already ranking it 331 in overall sales—which meant it was off to a tremendous start, and that a chart placing was very close. But the reaction to the free single offer back in November had really tipped everyone off to that already. The fans were out there, and they would be buying the album.

So how exactly could you top the achievements of 1999? Well, probably you couldn't, at least not in Britain.

You could only keep them going. But in other parts of the world, gradually achieving the same level of success they'd reached in the UK was the obvious goal. Think of it as getting the whole world to join the Club and be welcome at the party.

For each of them, life had changed beyond all recognition. In the course of two years they've gone from having regular jobs, temp jobs, just struggling, and flown all the way to the top. What was once "normal" seems like a luxury of free time now. But none of them would turn the clock back for anything. Well, who would when you're having such a great time, and seeing so much? Besides, you can always sleep later, right? You're only young once, so make the most of it, which is exactly what they're all doing. They've been able to rub shoulders with celebrities like the Corrs and the Eurythmics at Party In The Park, and Jo's had the chance to meet one of her idols, Bryan Adams, on *Top of the Pops*—not as a fan, but as an equal. It's all been pretty amazing, and it's really just begun.

CHAPTER SEVEN

MAGIC IS what it's about. The magic of capturing a crowd, whether it's through live performance, television, or on record. There are so many bands that try to do it, and so few who succeed. Yes, it's going to help if you have strong management and marketing behind you. But if you haven't got that ingredient X, then you might as well forget it. The Spice Girls had it, and look at the way they became globally huge. They were *alive*, they had real personalities that people could relate to, and they had a positive message. They weren't afraid of looking foolish and cartoonish at times. They became known equally as individuals, as well as part of the band, and that meant real success—they were instantly recognizable.

While there are a number of reasons why S Club 7 will probably never be quite as big as the Spice Girls—the main one being that the Girls were there before there was any competition in the teen market; there was time to get to know them—the goal is the one to aim for. And in a short time they've come a very long way, with top singles in Britain, a huge album, and a show that's now seen in forty-three countries. There's a good chance that the second season will be even more widely distributed, since it's set in Los Angeles, which to most outsiders really is America.

They've even attempted something no band has really done before—putting out their own S Club 7 magazine in the United States. During an S Club 7 marathon on Super Bowl Day 2000, there was an ad with an address where fans could write for a free edition of the magazine. It was a bold move. In the UK, it's not uncommon for official fan magazines to be available on the newsstands, but in America all the flow of teen information seems to come either through the regular teen magazines or the official fan clubs. But it seemed inevitable they'd be swamped with requests, if only because it *was* free. The last free offer made by the Club, for the single, had generated seven millions requests, after all. So someone— well, a lot of people—was watching.

Again, none of this guaranteed success. But they were willing to bide their time and let their fan base grow. The original plan had been to release *S Club* in the spring of 2000, fully half a year after the show had first aired. That was brought forward because of demand. And the series acted as their built-in promotion for the album, since most of the songs they performed on the telly were on the record. Everything interlocked very well and very cleverly. For a show that really hadn't been hyped, it had done very well to find its audience, especially on a Saturday morning schedule overflowing with programs aimed at kids.

What can never be overemphasized is the work that Tina, Bradley, Hannah, Jon, Rachel, Paul, and Jo have put into this. It's not their idea, not their songs, but they've really made it into something of their own. Even if they'd never paid their dues before, they're doing it now, with all the work they put in for the Club. It's a full-time job, in the very real sense of the phrase. And there's no clocking out at five P.M. to go and party the evenings or weekends away. From the moment they joined the Club, they've worked harder than they ever imagined was possible. Maybe it's a lot to ask of people, but they've all done it, and done it with big smiles on their faces. From starting out feeling they had a lot to prove, both to each other and the people who hired them, they've become totally absorbed in what they do. It's work, true, but how many people get to have this much fun while working?

The grueling days (and nights) become worthwhile when they can see what it is they were working on, on when thousands of fans join in the chorus of a song. There aren't many lines of work that offer the opportunity to get that massive kind of feedback, or the immediate energy and buzz of an audience.

They're lucky, and they've been lucky from the moment they were all selected to be a part of this very special thing. For some of them, this was exactly what they'd been working toward, a real shot at fame and fortune. For others, like Rachel, it was a happy coincidence of timing. But none of it would have happened if they hadn't all possessed the talent and the desire. For what they've achieved is something you really have to want, and be willing to do all it takes, endure the travel and sleepless night, to make it.

It's not the glamour-filled parties, or the photo shoots will all kinds of designer clothes. Those happen, but they're not what the life is all about. Basically, it's about work, very hard work, and developing a strong self-discipline to go with the drive. The Club might joke about Bradley being lazy and unable to get out of bed. But he's there, he's ready to go, and he's one of them.

For Rachel, John, Tina, Bradley, Jo, Paul, and Hannah, their lives have changed massively. No more lazing around on the weekend or going clubbing with their mates—and it's impossible for them not to miss that. But what they get instead makes it all worthwhile. Their dreams have all come true in ways they could never have imagined at the beginning of 1999.

It was an incredible year, but one that's only the beginning of the ride. It's going to become far madder as time goes by. Once they become huge in America it will *really* be insane. But that's fine; they'll be ready to handle it. By the very nature of things, they've learned a lot along the way. Fame isn't something everyone knows how to deal with. In fact, for some it's awful. You develop ways of handling it. One thing they all hope is that it doesn't reach the stage where they can't go out in public without bodyguards or disguises. They like being regular people, being just themselves, and it would be an awful price to pay if that had to change.

Hardly anyone is born famous, but there are those who seem destined for fame, and that's true of all the Club. Lots of kids dream of being actors on pop stars, but very few actually do anything to make that a reality. And not many have the talent to make it happen, either.

So will the Club still be together in five or ten years' time? There's not a really a yes or no answer to that. If things go well, then quite possibly they will. No one can predict the longevity of a band. Things happen, things change. But whatever way it goes, there's a major certainty that Jo will still be singing, and probably still scoring hits. Singing is just a natural part of who she is, it's what she was doing before she joined the club, and she'll be doing it for the rest of her life. And Paul, Hannah, and Jon will still be actors. It's their training, their background, and their major fulfillment.

Bradley will almost certainly be involved in music in some way. He might be singing—he does have that soulful voice, after all—or he might follow in his father's footsteps and open a recording studio (that's certainly one of his ultimate goals). Tina always has her dancing, and being known certainly won't hurt her in that, while Rachel could either continue singing or possibly even return to modeling.

In a lot of ways, whether the Club continue will depend on how satisfying everything is for all the members. At some point, they'll have to slow down or simply burn out. You can't keep going at that pace forever, and certainly not if you also want to have any kind of life. And at some point, they'll need to have lives. Maybe they'll take a sabbatical, the way the Spice Girls did, with a couple of them pursuing solo projects in music.

Without a crystal ball, predicting the future with any kind of certainty is impossible. But that's fine. If we knew what lay ahead, life wouldn't hold any surprises for us, and it's the twists and turns that make life so much fun for everyone.

Maybe music itself will change, and the emphasis will move from bands like S Club 7 to something else. It wouldn't be the first time something like that had happened, and it probably won't be the last, either.

But whatever does happen, in the here and now, S Club 7 are providing entertainment and great music, and that has to be the bottom line. Maybe, in another thirty years, they'll find themselves resurrected, the way the Monkees were, as great pop artifacts of an era.

Well, it's entirely possible, because they do make great pop music, and the shows are a great deal of fun. By the time the kids who are their fans today are parents, they'll have taken on the air of nostalgia.

Still, that's far in the future, well past a time anyone is thinking about. The bottom line is that, today, they're making catchy pop, putting on fantastic, energetic live performances, and have a funny, enjoyable show. And none of it resorts to sexual tactics, no crotch-grabbing or anything like that. Parents can feel good about their kids being into this band. They show you can be PG and very cool, which is something of a rarity, but a very welcome one.

They provide inspiration to a whole generation of kids. Nothing is impossible. In ten or fifteen years, one of them could be up there, and it might be because of the fever they caught watching S Club.

From England to Miami to Los Angeles, it's been a fast, crazy trip. In some ways it's been completely surreal for all seven of them, to the point where they still can't fully comprehend it. They have the platinum discs for their singles and album in the UK (which were actually presented live on a children's television show, *Blue Peter*), and they have the series and specials on video to prove they were there. But in the moment, while they're doing it, it's just life, and a great life at that.

They're bringing happiness and joy to a lot of people. Maybe it only lasts for the length of a song or a show, but it's still something very special. It's a gift, and one not given to many. To be able to make someone smile is a fabulous thing, to make them laugh and want to dance and forget whatever else is going on in their world.

Maybe their success won't last forever—very few things do. But while they're here, enjoy them to the fullest, and let yourself be touched by what they give you. Watch the show, sing along with the album, have a good time. That's what being in the Club is about—having fun. It's a guaranteed good time for all, and you'll leave there feeling a lot better than when you entered. From the UK to Miami, then Los Angeles, all the way to your house, the Club is coming for you, to offer you an invitation. There's room on the dance floor, and if you want to take a turn singing, that's fine, too. It's an S Club party, and everyone's going to be there. They hope you'll show up, too, and stay until it's all over.

GLOSSARY

YOU'VE PROBABLY noticed that while Brits and Americans more or less speak the same language, there's a distinct difference in the slang between the two countries. The members of S Club 7 definitely speak English, not American (and admit it, it's part of their charm, right?). So, in case you don't always get what they're talking about, here's a glossary of English slang to help you:

brilliant—excellent
cutesickle—cutie
deffo—definitely
love puff—cutie
mad—crazy but good, as in "we had a mad time"
mate(s)—your close friend(s)
mental—like mad, but even crazier
obv—obviously
parp—utter garbage
plonker—a useless person
pulling the blokes—getting a date with a guy
to rubbish—to put someone or something down verbally
snogging—necking

top—the best, as in a top night out

totty—a person of the opposite sex, especially if he/she
   is attractive

twonk—like a plonker

well—extremely, as if that experience was well-weird

DISCOGRAPHY

UK Singles

"Bring It All Back/So Right" (1999)	Highest Chart Position #1
"S Club Party" (1999)	Highest Chart Position #1
"You're My Number One/ Two In A Million" (1999)	Highest Chart Position #2

UK Albums

S Club (1999)	Highest Chart Position #1

S Club 7 also appear on

Children's Promise—"It's Only Rock 'n' Roll" (1999)

U.S. Singles

"Bring It All Back" (1999)

U.S. Albums

S Club (2000)

HOME VIDEO

It's an S Club Thing (1999, UK only)

WEBSITES

THESE DAYS everyone has a website, or so it seems. And if you're famous, you have the official one, plus any number of unofficial sites put together by fans. Well, S Club are famous, so they definitely fall into the latter category.

The place to start is with the official site, *www.sclub7.co.uk*—it offers you two choices, the British or American. The American side will tell you that the show appears on Fox Family, and when, but that's about the size of it. The British side, however, is an amazing site, once you've waited a few minutes for it to fully load. You'll also need Flash, which is a free browser plug-in, downloadable through the site, but which you might already have on your computer. Lots of information about each of the band members, the series, their records, and the charities they support. And there are also some great outtake photos from the series. All in all, it's one of the best official sites around, even though it needs to be updated a little more often.

The fan sites, of course, don't generally have access to the time and technology, so by their nature they tend to be a little more simple. But they're still all done with love.

Jayme's S Club 7 site (*welcome.to/s_club_7*) is fairly basic, but offers the information you need to learn about the guys and girls, and a good selection of pictures.

Dedicated to S Club 7 (*www.starfleet6.freeserve.co. uk*) is exactly what it claims to be. Again, it's fairly limited in its scope—none of the sites reprint any articles, by the way—but it serves as an excellent introduction.

If you know that you like the girls, then Girls of S Club 7 (*www.girlssc7.cjb.net*) is a site you need to visit. Even though, at the time of writing, it was going to be upgraded with Flash, it was still very impressive. Lots of pictures, not only publicity shots, but also from the show, and from both the television specials. A good place to satisfy that Jo, Tina, Hannah, or Rachel hunger.

Listen To S Club 7 (*www.listen.to/sclub7*) doesn't really give you a chance to actually listen to them. Again, it's a good introductory site, full of the basics, but it has the potential to develop into more.

Much the same can be said of S Club 7 Fan Central (*go.to/sclub7*), which, at the time of my visit, needed some updating. But if you want to see what the Club were like in 1999, the year they hit big, these places are fine.

The S Club 7 Unoffical Site (*www.sclub7online.co.uk*) proved to be a real treasure trove. Not only did it contain an excellent news section, picture gallery, and so on, but there were also MP3s available, as well as a selection of S Club merchandise, for those who simply have to own the tee shirt or the cap. It was thorough, and laid out in an incredibly professional manner.

It's true that a lot of the sites seem more like exercises in making a website than something to keep up with the band. But before you start thinking that some sites are no good, not worth the bother, maybe you should remember that people have put a lot of time and effort into making these things in the first place. Every one is an achievement, and should be treated that way, with plenty of respect. And, if you believe you can do better, then go ahead—make your own S Club 7 unofficial site. The more the merrier. Make it the best you can, and along the way you'll have learned a great deal, not only in skills, but about yourself and the Club. If you want to, you can manage it—nothing is impossible. We can do it—remember?